The *New* Daily Study Bible

The Revelation
of John

Volume 1

The *New* Daily Study Bible

The Revelation of John

Volume I

William Barclay

SAINT ANDREW PRESS
Edinburgh

Published by
SAINT ANDREW PRESS
121 George Street, Edinburgh EH2 4YN

© The William Barclay Estate, 1976, 2004

First edition published in 1959 as *The Daily Study Bible: The Revelation of John*
Revised edition published in 1976
This third edition fully revised and updated by Saint Andrew Press and published as
The New Daily Study Bible: The Revelation of John in 2004

The Scripture quotations contained herein are from The New Revised Standard Version of the Bible, Anglicized Edition, copyright © 1989, 1995 by the Division of Christian Education of the National Council of the Churches of Christ in the United States of America, and are used by permission. All rights reserved.

ISBN 0 7152 0795 4

The right of William Barclay to be identified as author of this work has been asserted according to the Copyright, Designs and Patents Act, 1988.

British Library Cataloguing in Publication Data
A CIP record for this book is available from the British Library

Cover design by McColl Productions Ltd, by courtesy of Saint Andrew Press

All rights reserved. No part of this publication may be reproduced or transmitted in any form or by any means, electronic or mechanical, including photocopy, recording, or information storage and retrieval system, without permission in writing from the publisher. This book is sold subject to the condition that it shall not, by way of trade or otherwise, be lent, re-sold, hired out or otherwise circulated without the publisher's prior consent.

Typeset by Waverley Typesetters, Galashiels
Printed in Great Britain by Creative Print & Design, Wales

To

ALL THOSE READERS

WHO BEGAN WITH ME

AT THE BEGINNING OF THIS SERIES

AND WHO HAVE PERSEVERED WITH ME

TO THIS THE END

CONTENTS

REVELATION

REVELATION

REVELATION

SERIES FOREWORD
(by Ronnie Barclay)

My father always had a great love for the English language and its literature. As a student at the University of Glasgow, he won a prize in the English class – and I have no doubt that he could have become a Professor of English instead of Divinity and Biblical Criticism. In a pre-computer age, he had a mind like a computer that could store vast numbers of quotations, illustrations, anecdotes and allusions; and, more remarkably still, he could retrieve them at will. The editor of this revision has, where necessary, corrected and attributed the vast majority of these quotations with considerable skill and has enhanced our pleasure as we read quotations from Plato to T. S. Eliot.

There is another very welcome improvement in the new text. My mother was one of five sisters, and my grandmother was a commanding figure as the Presbyterian minister's wife in a small village in Ayrshire in Scotland. She ran that small community very efficiently, and I always felt that my father, surrounded by so many women, was more than somewhat overawed by it all! I am sure that this is the reason why his use of English tended to be dominated by the words 'man', 'men' and so on, with the result that it sounded very male-orientated. Once again, the editor has very skilfully improved my father's English and made the text much more readable for all of us by amending the often one-sided language.

It is a well-known fact that William Barclay wrote at break-neck speed and never corrected anything once it was on paper – he took great pride in mentioning this at every possible opportunity! This revision, in removing repetition and correcting the inevitable errors that had slipped through, has produced a text free from all the tell-tale signs of very rapid writing. It is with great pleasure that I commend this revision to readers old and new in the certainty that William Barclay speaks even more clearly to us all with his wonderful appeal in this new version of his much-loved *Daily Study Bible*.

Ronnie Barclay
Bedfordshire
2001

GENERAL INTRODUCTION

(by William Barclay, from the 1975 edition)

The Daily Study Bible series has always had one aim – to convey the results of scholarship to the ordinary reader. A. S. Peake delighted in the saying that he was a 'theological middle-man', and I would be happy if the same could be said of me in regard to these volumes. And yet the primary aim of the series has never been academic. It could be summed up in the famous words of Richard of Chichester's prayer – to enable men and women 'to know Jesus Christ more clearly, to love him more dearly, and to follow him more nearly'.

It is all of twenty years since the first volume of *The Daily Study Bible* was published. The series was the brain-child of the late Rev. Andrew McCosh, MA, STM, the then Secretary and Manager of the Committee on Publications of the Church of Scotland, and of the late Rev. R. G. Macdonald, OBE, MA, DD, its Convener.

It is a great joy to me to know that all through the years *The Daily Study Bible* has been used at home and abroad, by minister, by missionary, by student and by layman, and that it has been translated into many different languages. Now, after so many printings, it has become necessary to renew the printer's type and the opportunity has been taken to restyle the books, to correct some errors in the text and to remove some references which have become outdated. At the same time, the Biblical quotations within the text have been changed to use the Revised Standard Version, but my own original translation of the New Testament passages has been retained at the beginning of each daily section.

There is one debt which I would be sadly lacking in courtesy if I did not acknowledge. The work of revision and correction has been done entirely by the Rev. James Martin, MA, BD, Minister of High Carntyne Church, Glasgow. Had it not been for him this task would never have been undertaken, and it is impossible for me to thank him enough for the selfless toil he has put into the revision of these books.

It is my prayer that God may continue to use *The Daily Study Bible* to enable men better to understand His word.

William Barclay
Glasgow
1975
(Published in the 1975 edition)

GENERAL FOREWORD

(by John Drane)

I only met William Barclay once, not long after his retirement from the chair of Biblical Criticism at the University of Glasgow. Of course I had known about him long before that, not least because his theological passion – the Bible – was also a significant formative influence in my own life and ministry. One of my most vivid memories of his influence goes back to when I was working on my own doctoral research in the New Testament. It was summer 1971, and I was a leader on a mission team working in the north-east of Scotland at the same time as Barclay's Baird Lectures were being broadcast on national television. One night, a young Ph.D. scientist who was interested in Christianity, but still unsure about some things, came to me and announced: 'I've just been watching William Barclay on TV. He's convinced me that I need to be a Christian; when can I be baptized?' That kind of thing did not happen every day. So how could it be that Barclay's message was so accessible to people with no previous knowledge or experience of the Christian faith?

I soon realised that there was no magic ingredient that enabled this apparently ordinary professor to be a brilliant communicator. His secret lay in who he was, his own sense of identity and purpose, and above all his integrity in being true to himself and his faith. Born in the far north of Scotland, he was brought up in Motherwell, a steel-producing town south of Glasgow where his family settled when he was only five, and this was the kind of place where he felt most at home. Though his association with the University of Glasgow provided a focus for his life over almost fifty years, from his first day as a student in 1925 to his retirement from the faculty in 1974, he never became an ivory-tower academic, divorced from the realities of life in the real world. On the contrary, it was his commitment to the working-class culture of industrial Clydeside that enabled him to make such a lasting contribution not only to the world of the university but also to the life of the Church.

He was ordained to the ministry of the Church of Scotland at the age of twenty-six, but was often misunderstood even by other Christians. I doubt that William Barclay would ever have chosen words such as 'missionary' or 'evangelist' to describe his own ministry, but he accomplished what few others have done, as he took the traditional Presbyterian emphasis on spirituality-through-learning and transformed it into a most effective vehicle for evangelism. His own primary interest was in the history and language of the New Testament, but William Barclay was never only a historian or literary critic. His constant concern was to explore how these ancient books, and the faith of which they spoke, could continue to be relevant to people of his own time. If the Scottish churches had known how to capitalize on his enormous popularity in the media during the 1960s and 1970s, they might easily have avoided much of the decline of subsequent years.

Connecting the Bible to life has never been the way to win friends in the world of academic theology, and Barclay could undoubtedly have made things easier for himself had he been prepared to be a more conventional academic. But he was too deeply rooted in his own culture – and too seriously committed to the gospel – for that. He could see little purpose in a belief system that was so wrapped up in arcane and complicated terminology that it was accessible only to experts. Not only did he demystify Christian theology, but he also did it for working people, addressing the kind of things that mattered to ordinary folks in their everyday lives. In doing so, he also challenged the elitism that has often been deeply ingrained in the twin worlds of academic theology and the Church, with their shared assumption that popular culture is an inappropriate vehicle for serious thinking. Professor Barclay can hardly have been surprised when his predilection for writing books for the masses – not to mention talking to them on television – was questioned by his peers and even occasionally dismissed as being 'unscholarly' or insufficiently 'academic'. That was all untrue, of course, for his work was soundly based in reliable scholarship and his own extensive knowledge of the original languages of the Bible. But like One many centuries before him (and unlike most of his peers, in both Church and academy), 'the common people heard him gladly' (Mark 12:37), which no doubt explains why his writings are still inspirational – and why it is a particular pleasure for me personally to commend them to a new readership in a new century.

John Drane
University of Aberdeen
2001

EDITOR'S PREFACE

(by Linda Foster)

When the first volume of the original *Daily Bible Readings*, which later became *The Daily Study Bible* (the commentary on Acts), was published in 1953, no one could have anticipated or envisaged the revolution in the use of language which was to take place in the last quarter of the twentieth century. Indeed, when the first revised edition, to which William Barclay refers in his General Introduction, was completed in 1975, such a revolution was still waiting in the wings. But at the beginning of the twenty-first century, inclusive language and the concept of political correctness are well-established facts of life. It has therefore been with some trepidation that the editing of this unique and much-loved text has been undertaken in producing *The New Daily Study Bible*. Inevitably, the demands of the new language have resulted in the loss of some of Barclay's most sonorous phrases, perhaps best remembered in the often-repeated words 'many a man'. Nonetheless, this revision is made in the conviction that William Barclay, the great communicator, would have welcomed it. In the discussion of Matthew 9:16–17 ('The Problem of the New Idea'), he affirmed the value of language that has stood the test of time and in which people have 'found comfort and put their trust', but he also spoke of 'living in a changing and expanding world' and questioned the wisdom of reading God's word to twentieth-century men and women in Elizabethan English. It is the intention of this new edition to heed that warning and to bring

William Barclay's message of God's word to readers of the twenty-first century in the language of their own time.

In the editorial process, certain decisions have been made in order to keep a balance between that new language and the familiar Barclay style. Quotations from the Bible are now taken from the New Revised Standard Version, but William Barclay's own translation of individual passages has been retained throughout. Where the new version differs from the text on which Barclay originally commented, because of the existence of an alternative reading, the variant text is indicated by square brackets. I have made no attempt to guess what Barclay would have said about the NRSV text; his commentary still refers to the Authorized (King James) and Revised Standard Versions of the Bible, but I believe that the inclusive language of the NRSV considerably assists the flow of the discussion.

For similar reasons, the dating conventions of BC and AD – rather than the more recent and increasingly used BCE (before the common era) and CE (common era) – have been retained. William Barclay took great care to explain the meanings of words and phrases and scholarly points, but it has not seemed appropriate to select new terms and make such explanations on his behalf.

One of the most difficult problems to solve has concerned monetary values. Barclay had his own system for translating the coinage of New Testament times into British currency. Over the years, these equivalent values have become increasingly out of date, and often the force of the point being made has been lost or diminished. There is no easy way to bring these equivalents up to date in a way that will continue to make sense, particularly when readers come from both sides of the Atlantic. I have therefore followed the only known yardstick that gives any feel for the values concerned, namely that a *denarius* was a day's wage for a working man, and I have made alterations to the text accordingly.

One of the striking features of *The Daily Study Bible* is the range of quotations from literature and hymnody that are used by way of illustration. Many of these passages appeared without identification or attribution, and for the new edition I have attempted wherever possible to provide sources and authors. In the same way, details have been included about scholars and other individuals cited, by way of context and explanation, and I am most grateful to Professor John Drane for his assistance in discovering information about some of the more obscure or unfamiliar characters. It is clear that readers use *The Daily Study Bible* in different ways. Some look up particular passages while others work through the daily readings in a more systematic way. The descriptions and explanations are therefore not offered every time an individual is mentioned (in order to avoid repetition that some may find tedious), but I trust that the information can be discovered without too much difficulty.

Finally, the 'Further Reading' lists at the end of each volume have been removed. Many new commentaries and individual studies have been added to those that were the basis of William Barclay's work, and making a selection from that ever-increasing catalogue is an impossible task. It is nonetheless my hope that the exploration that begins with these volumes of *The New Daily Study Bible* will go on in the discovery of new writers and new books.

Throughout the editorial process, many conversations have taken place – conversations with the British and American publishers, and with those who love the books and find in them both information and inspiration. Ronnie Barclay's contribution to this revision of his father's work has been invaluable. But one conversation has dominated the work, and that has been a conversation with William Barclay himself through the text. There has been a real sense of listening to his voice in all the questioning and in the searching for new words to convey the meaning of that text. The aim of *The New Daily Study Bible* is to make clear his message, so that the distinctive voice, which has spoken to so many in past years, may continue to be heard for generations to come.

Linda Foster
London
2001

INTRODUCTION TO THE REVELATION OF JOHN

The Strange Book

When we embark upon the study of Revelation, we feel ourselves projected into a different world. Here is something quite unlike the rest of the New Testament. Not only is Revelation different; it is also notoriously difficult to understand. The result is that it has sometimes been abandoned as quite unintelligible and it has sometimes become the playground of religious eccentrics, who use it to map out celestial timetables of what is to come or who find in it evidence for their own eccentricities. One despairing commentator said that there are as many riddles in Revelation as there are words, and another that the study of Revelation either finds or leaves the reader mad.

The founder of the Protestant Reformation, Martin Luther, would have denied Revelation a place in the New Testament. Along with James, Jude, 2 Peter and Hebrews, he relegated it to a separate list at the end of his New Testament. He declared that in it there are only images and visions such as are found nowhere else in the Bible. He complained that, notwithstanding the obscurity of his writing, the writer had the boldness to add threats and promises for those who disobeyed or kept his words, unintelligible though they were. In it, said Luther, Christ is neither taught nor acknowledged; and the inspiration of the Holy Spirit is not perceptible in it. Another Reformation scholar, Huldreich Zwingli, is equally hostile to Revelation. 'With the Apocalypse,' he writes, 'we have no concern, for it is not a biblical book ... The Apocalypse has no savour of the mouth or the mind of John. I can, if I so will, reject its testimonies.' Most voices have stressed the unintelligibility of Revelation, and not a few have questioned its right to a place in the New Testament.

On the other hand, there are those in every generation who have loved this book. In his commentary, T. S. Kepler quotes the verdict of the early Church historian and Archbishop of Quebec, Philip Carrington, and makes it his own: 'In the case of Revelation, we are dealing with an artist greater than Stevenson or Coleridge or Bach. St John has a better sense of the right word than Stevenson; he has a greater command of unearthly supernatural loveliness than Coleridge; he has a richer sense of melody and rhythm and composition than Bach ... It is the only masterpiece of pure art in the New Testament ... Its fulness and richness and harmonic variety place it far above Greek tragedy.'

We shall no doubt find this book difficult and bewildering; but doubtless, too, we shall find it infinitely worth while to wrestle with it until it gives us its blessing and opens its riches to us.

Apocalyptic Literature

In any study of Revelation, we must begin by remembering the basic fact that, although unique in the New Testament, it is nonetheless representative of a kind of literature which was the most common of all in the period between the Old and the New Testaments. Revelation is commonly called the Apocalypse – in Greek *apokalupsis*. Between the Old and the New Testaments, there grew up a great mass of what is called apocalyptic literature, the product of an indestructible Jewish hope.

The Jews could not forget that they were the chosen people of God. To them, that involved the certainty that some day they would arrive at world supremacy. In their early history, they looked forward to the coming of a king of David's line who would unite the nation and lead them to greatness. A shoot was to come forth from the stump of Jesse (Isaiah 11:1, 11:10). God would raise up a righteous branch for David (Jeremiah 23:5). Some day, the people would serve David, their king (Jeremiah 30:9). David would be their shepherd and their king (Ezekiel 34:23, 37:24). The booth of David would be repaired (Amos 9:11); out of Bethlehem there would come a ruler who would be great to the ends of the earth (Micah 5:2–4).

But the whole history of Israel contradicted these hopes. After the death of Solomon, the kingdom – small enough to begin with – split into two under Rehoboam and Jeroboam, and so lost its unity. The northern kingdom, with its capital at Samaria, vanished in the last quarter of the eighth century BC before the assault of the Assyrians, never again reappeared in history and is now referred to as the lost ten tribes. The southern kingdom, with its capital at Jerusalem, was reduced to slavery and exile by the Babylonians in the early part of the sixth century BC. It later came under the rule of the Persians, the Greeks and finally the Romans. History for the Jews was a catalogue of disasters from which it became clear that no human deliverer could rescue them.

The Two Ages

Jewish thought stubbornly held to the conviction of the chosenness of the Jews but had to adjust itself to the facts of history. It did so by working out a scheme of history. The Jews divided all time into two ages. There was *this present age*, which is wholly bad and beyond redemption. For it, there can be nothing but total destruction. The Jews, therefore, waited for the end of things as they are. There was *the age which is to come*, which was to be wholly good, the golden age of God, in which would be peace, prosperity and righteousness, and the place of God's chosen people would at last be upheld as theirs by right.

How was this present age to become the age which is to come? The Jews believed that the change could never be brought about by human agency and, therefore, looked for the direct intervention of God. He would come striding on to the stage of history to blast this present world out of existence and bring in his golden time. The day of the coming of God was called the day of the Lord and was to be a terrible time of fear and destruction and judgment, which would be the signs of the coming new age.

All apocalyptic literature deals with these events – the sin of the present age, the terrors of the time between, and the blessings of the time to come. It is entirely composed of dreams and visions of the end. That means that all apocalyptic literature is inevitably cryptic. It is continually attempting to describe the indescribable, to say the unsayable and to paint the unpaintable.

This is further complicated by another fact. It was only natural that these apocalyptic visions should flame the more brightly in the minds of people living under tyranny and oppression. The more some alien power held them down, the more they dreamed of the destruction of that power and of their own recognition and restoration. But it would only have worsened the situation if the oppressing power could have understood these dreams. Such writings would have seemed the works of rebellious revolutionaries. These books, there-fore, were frequently written in code, deliberately couched in language which was unintelligible to the outsider; and inevitably there are many cases in which they remain unintelligible because the key to the code no longer exists. But the more we know about the historical background of such books, the better we can interpret them.

The Book of Revelation

All this is the precise picture of our Revelation. There are any number of Jewish apocalypses – Enoch, the Sibylline Oracles, the Testaments of the Twelve Patriarchs, the Ascension of Isaiah, the Assumption of Moses, the Apocalypse of Baruch, 4 Ezra. Our Revelation is a Christian apocalypse. It is the only one in the New Testament, although there were many other similar writings which did not gain admission. It is written exactly on the Jewish pattern and follows the basic idea of the two ages. The only difference is that, for the day of the Lord, it substitutes the coming in power of Jesus Christ. Not only the pattern but also the details are the same. The Jewish apocalypses had a standard sequence of events which were to happen at the last time; these events all have their place in Revelation.

Before we go on to outline that pattern of events, another question arises. Both *apocalyptic* and *prophecy* deal with the events which are to come. What, then, is the difference between them?

Apocalyptic and Prophecy

The difference between the prophets and the writers of apocalyptic was very real. There were two main differences – one of message and one of method.

(1) The prophets thought in terms of this present world. Their message was often a cry for social, economic and political justice, and was always a summons to obey and

serve God within this present world. To the prophets, it was this world which was to be reformed and in which God's kingdom would come. This has been expressed by saying that the prophets believed in history. They believed that, in the events of history, God's purpose was being worked out. In one sense, the prophets were optimists – for, however sternly they condemned the present state of affairs, they nonetheless believed that things could be put right if men and women would accept the will of God. To the apocalyptists, the world was beyond help in the present. They believed not in the reformation but in the destruction of this present world. They looked forward to the creation of a new world when this one had been shattered by the avenging wrath of God. In one sense, therefore, the apocalyptists were pessimists, for they did not believe that things as they were could ever be cured. True, they were quite certain that the golden age would come – but only after this world had been destroyed.

(2) The message of the prophets was spoken; the message of the apocalyptists was always written. Apocalyptic is a literary production. Had it been delivered by word of mouth, people would never have understood it. It is difficult, involved, often unintelligible; it has to be pored over before it can be understood. Further, the prophets always spoke under their own names; but all apocalyptic writings – except our New Testament one – are pseudonymous. They are put into the mouths of great ones of the past, like Noah, Enoch, Isaiah, Moses, the Twelve Patriarchs, Ezra and Baruch. There is something rather sad about this. Those who wrote the apocalyptic literature had the feeling that greatness had gone from the earth; they did not have the confidence in their own position and authority to put their names to their works, and attributed them to the great figures of the past, thereby seeking

to give them an authority greater than their own names could have given. As the New Testament scholar Adolf Jülicher put it: 'Apocalyptic is prophecy turned senile.'

The Pattern of Apocalyptic

Apocalyptic literature has a pattern: it seeks to describe the things which will happen at the last times and the blessedness which will follow; and the same pictures occur over and over again. It always, so to speak, worked with the same materials; and these materials find their place in our Book of Revelation.

(1) In apocalyptic literature, the Messiah was a divine, pre-existent, other-worldly figure of power and glory, waiting to descend into the world to begin his all-conquering career. He existed in heaven before the creation of the world, before the sun and the stars were made; and he is preserved in the presence of the Almighty (1 Enoch 48:3, 48:6, 62:7; 4 Ezra 13:25–6). He will come to put down the mighty from their seats, to dethrone the kings of the earth and to break the teeth of sinners (1 Enoch 42:2–6, 48:2–9, 62:5–9, 69:26–9). In apocalyptic, there was nothing human or gentle about the Messiah; he was a divine figure of avenging power and glory before whom the earth trembled in terror.

(2) The coming of the Messiah was to be preceded by the return of Elijah, who would prepare the way for him (Malachi 4:5–6). Elijah was to stand upon the hills of Israel, so the Rabbis said, and announce the coming of the Messiah with a voice so great that it would sound from one end of the earth to the other.

(3) The last terrible times were known as 'the travail of the Messiah'. The coming of the messianic age would be like the agony of birth. In the gospels, Jesus is depicted as

foretelling the signs of the end and is reported as saying: 'All this is but the beginning of the birth pangs' (Matthew 24:8; Mark 13:8).

(4) The last days will be a time of terror. Even the mighty will cry bitterly (Zephaniah 1:14); the inhabitants of the land shall tremble (Joel 2:1); people will be terrified and will seek some place to hide and will find none (1 Enoch 102:1, 102:3).

(5) The last days will be a time when the world will be shattered, a time of cosmic upheaval when the universe, as we know it, will disintegrate. The stars will be extinguished; the sun will be turned into darkness and the moon into blood (Isaiah 13:10; Joel 2:30–1, 3:15). The firmament will crash in ruins; there will be a torrent of raging fire, and creation will become a molten mass (Sibylline Oracles 3:83–9). The seasons will lose their order, and there will be neither night nor dawn (Sibylline Oracles 3:796–806).

(6) The last days will be a time when human relationships will be destroyed. Hatred and enmity will reign upon the earth. People will turn against their neighbours (Zechariah 14:13). Brothers will kill each other; parents will murder their own children; from dawn to sunset they shall slay one another (1 Enoch 100:1–2). Honour will be turned into shame, strength into humiliation, and beauty into ugliness. Jealousy will arise in those who did not think much of themselves, and passion will take hold of those who were peaceful (2 Baruch 48:31–7).

(7) The last days will be a time of judgment. God will come like a refiner's fire – and who can endure the day of his coming (Malachi 3:1–3)? It is by the fire and the sword that God will plead with people (Isaiah 66:15–16). The Son of Man will destroy sinners from the earth (1 Enoch 69:27), and the smell of brimstone will pervade all things (Sibylline Oracles

3:58–61). The sinners will be burned up as Sodom was long ago (Jubilees 36:10–11).

(8) In all these visions, the Gentiles have their place – but it is not always the same place.

(a) Sometimes the vision is that the Gentiles will be totally destroyed. Babylon will become such a desolation that there will be no place for the wandering Arabs to plant their tents among the ruins, no place for the shepherds to graze their sheep; it will be nothing more than a desert inhabited by the beasts (Isaiah 13:19–22). God will trample down the Gentiles in his anger (Isaiah 63:6). The Gentiles will come over in chains to Israel (Isaiah 45:14).

(b) Sometimes one last gathering of the Gentiles against Jerusalem is depicted, and one last battle in which they are destroyed (Ezekiel 38:14–39:16; Zechariah 14:1–11). The kings of the nations will throw themselves against Jerusalem; they will seek to ravage the shrine of the Holy One; they will place their thrones in a ring round the city, with their faithless people with them; but it will be only for their final destruction (Sibylline Oracles 3:663–72).

(c) Sometimes there is the picture of the conversion of the Gentiles through Israel. God has given Israel as a light to the Gentiles, that God's salvation may reach to the ends of the earth (Isaiah 49:6). The coastlands wait upon God (Isaiah 51:5); the ends of the earth are invited to look to God and be saved (Isaiah 45:20–2). The Son of Man will be a light to the Gentiles (1 Enoch 48:4–5). Nations shall come from the ends of the earth to Jerusalem to see the glory of God (Psalms of Solomon 17:31).

Of all the pictures in connection with the Gentiles, the most common is that of the destruction of the Gentiles and the exaltation of Israel.

(9) In the last days, the Jews who have been scattered throughout the earth will be gathered into the holy city again. They will come back from Assyria and from Egypt and will worship the Lord in his holy mountain (Isaiah 27:12–13). The hills will be removed and the valleys will be filled in, and even the trees will gather to give them shade as they come back (Baruch 5:5–9). Even those who died as exiles in far countries will be brought back.

(10) In the last days, the New Jerusalem, which is already prepared in heaven with God (4 Ezra 10:44–59; 2 Baruch 4:2–6), will come down among men and women. It will be more beautiful than anything else, with foundations of sapphires, pinnacles of agate, and jewelled gates on walls of precious stones (Isaiah 54:11–12; Tobit 13:16). The glory of the latter house will be greater than the glory of the former (Haggai 2:9).

(11) An essential part of the apocalyptic picture of the last days was the resurrection of the dead. 'Many of those who sleep in the dust of the earth shall awake, some to everlasting life, and some to shame and everlasting contempt' (Daniel 12:2–3). Sheol and the grave will give back that which has been entrusted to them (1 Enoch 51:1). The scope of the resurrection of the dead varied. Sometimes it was to apply only to the righteous in Israel; sometimes to all Israel; and sometimes to all people everywhere. Whatever form it took, it is true to say that now for the first time we see emerging a strong hope of a life beyond the grave.

(12) There were differences as to how long the messianic kingdom was to last. The most natural – and the most usual – view was to think of it as lasting forever. The kingdom of the saints is an everlasting kingdom (Daniel 7:27). Some believed that the reign of the Messiah would last for 400 years. They arrived at this figure from a comparison of

Genesis 15:13 and Psalm 90:15. In Genesis, Abraham is told that the period of affliction of the children of Israel will be 400 years; the psalmist's prayer is that God will make the nation glad for as many days as he has afflicted them and as many years as they have seen evil. In Revelation, the view is that there is to be a reign of the saints for 1,000 years; then the final battle with the assembled powers of evil; then the golden age of God.

Such were the events which the apocalyptic writers pictured in the last days; and practically all of them find their place in the pictures of Revelation. To complete the picture, we may briefly summarize the blessings of the coming age.

The Blessings of the Age to Come

(1) The divided kingdom will be united again. The house of Judah will walk again with the house of Israel (Jeremiah 3:18; Isaiah 11:13; Hosea 1:11). The old divisions will be healed, and the people of God will be one.

(2) There will be in the world an amazing fertility. The wilderness will become a field (Isaiah 32:15); it will become like the garden of Eden (Isaiah 51:3); the desert will rejoice and blossom like the crocus (Isaiah 35:1). The earth will yield its fruit ten thousandfold; on each vine will be 1,000 branches, on each branch 1,000 clusters, in each cluster 1,000 grapes, and each grape will give a cor (120 gallons) of wine (2 Baruch 29:5–8). There will be a situation of plenty, such as the world has never known, and the hungry will rejoice.

(3) A consistent part of the dream of the new age was that in it all wars would cease. The swords will be beaten into ploughshares and the spears into pruning-hooks (Isaiah 2:4). There will be no sword or noise of battle. There will be a common law for everyone and a great peace throughout the

earth, and king will be friendly with king (Sibylline Oracles 3:751–60).

(4) One of the loveliest ideas concerning the new age was that in it there would be no more conflict between wild animals or between human beings and the animal world. The leopard and the kid, the cow and the bear, the lion and the calf will play and lie down together (Isaiah 11:6–9, 65:25). There will be a new covenant between human beings and all living creatures (Hosea 2:18). Even a child will be able to play where the poisonous reptiles have their holes and their dens (Isaiah 11:6–9; 2 Baruch 73:6). In all nature, there will be a universal reign of friendship in which none will wish to do another any harm.

(5) The coming age will bring the end of weariness, of sorrow and of pain. The people will not faint or pine any more (Jeremiah 31:12); everlasting joy will be upon their heads (Isaiah 35:10). There will be no such thing as an untimely death (Isaiah 65:20–2); no one will say: 'I am sick' (Isaiah 33:24); death will be swallowed up, and God will wipe tears from all faces (Isaiah 25:8). Disease will withdraw; anxiety, anguish and lamentation will pass away; childbirth will have no pain; the reaper will not grow weary and the builder will not be toilworn (2 Baruch 73:2–74:4). The age to come will be one when what the Roman poet Virgil called 'the tears of things' will be no more.

(6) The age to come will be an age of righteousness. There will be perfect holiness among human beings. This generation will be a good generation, living in the fear of the Lord in the days of mercy (Psalms of Solomon 17:28–49, 18:9–10).

The Book of Revelation is the New Testament representative of all these apocalyptic works which tell of the terrors before the end of time and of the blessings of the age to come; and it uses all the familiar imagery. It may often be difficult and even unintelligible to us; but, for the most part, it was using pictures and ideas which those who read it would have known and understood.

The Author of Revelation

(1) Revelation was written by a man called John. He begins by saying that God sent the visions he is going to relate to his servant John (1:1). The main body of the book begins with the statement that it is from John to the seven churches in Asia (1:4). 'I, John,' he says, 'am the one who heard and saw these things' (22:8).

(2) This John was a Christian who lived in Asia in the same sphere as the Christians of the seven churches. He calls himself the brother of those to whom he writes; and he says that he too shares in the tribulations through which they are passing (1:9).

(3) He was most probably a Jew of Palestine who had come to Asia Minor late in life. We can deduce this from the kind of Greek that he writes. It is vivid, powerful and pictorial, but from the point of view of grammar it is easily the worst Greek in the New Testament. He makes mistakes which even those with only a basic knowledge of Greek would never make. Greek is certainly not his native language; and it is often clear that he is writing in Greek and thinking in Hebrew. He has a detailed knowledge of the Old Testament. He quotes it or alludes to it 245 times. These quotations come from about twenty Old Testament books; his favourites are Isaiah, Daniel, Ezekiel, Psalms, Exodus, Jeremiah and Zechariah. Not only does he know the Old Testament intimately; he is also familiar with the apocalyptic books written between the Testaments.

(4) His claim for himself is that he is a prophet, and it is on that fact that he bases his right to speak. The command of the risen Christ to him is that he must prophesy (10:11). It is

through the spirit of prophecy that Jesus gives his witness to the Church (19:10). God is the God of the holy prophets and sends his angel to show his servants what is going to happen in the world (22:6). The angel speaks to him of his brothers the prophets (22:9). His book is characteristically prophecy or the words of prophecy (22:7, 22:10, 22:18–19).

It is here that John's authority lies. He does not call himself an apostle, as Paul does when he wants to underline his right to speak. He has no 'official' or administrative position in the Church; he is a prophet. He writes what he sees; and, since what he sees comes from God, his word is faithful and true (1:11, 1:19).

When John was writing, the prophets had a very special place in the Church. He was writing, as we shall see, in about AD 90. By that time, the Church had two kinds of ministry. There was the local ministry; those engaged in it were settled permanently in one congregation as the elders, the deacons and the teachers. There was also the travelling ministry of those whose sphere of work was not confined to any one congregation. In it were the apostles, whose authority ran throughout the whole Church; and there were the prophets, who were wandering preachers. The prophets were greatly respected; the *Didache* says (11:7) that to question the words of a true prophet was to sin against the Holy Spirit. The accepted order of service for the celebration of the Eucharist is laid down in the *Didache*, but at the end comes the sentence: 'But allow the prophets to hold the Eucharist as they will' (10:7). The prophets were regarded as uniquely coming from God; and John was a prophet.

(5) It is unlikely that he was an apostle. Otherwise, he would hardly have put such emphasis on the fact that he was a prophet. Further, he speaks of the apostles as if he was looking back on them as the great foundations of the Church. He speaks of the twelve foundations of the wall of the holy city, and then says:

'and on them were the twelve names of the twelve apostles of the Lamb' (21:14). He would scarcely have spoken of the apostles like that if he himself had been one of them.

This conclusion is made even more likely by the title of the book. In the Authorized and Revised Versions, it is called *the Revelation of St John the Divine*. In the Revised Standard Version and in James Moffatt's and in J. B. Phillips' translations, *the Divine* is omitted, because it is absent from the majority of the oldest Greek manuscripts; but it does go a long way back. The Greek is *theologos*, and the word is used here in the sense in which scholars speak of 'the Puritan divines'. It means not John the saintly but John the theologian; and the very addition of that title seems to distinguish this John from the John who was the apostle.

As long ago as AD 250, Dionysius, the great scholar who was head of the Christian school at Alexandria, saw that it was well nigh impossible that the same man could have written both Revelation and the Fourth Gospel, if for no other reason than that the Greek is so different. The Greek of the Fourth Gospel is simple but correct; the Greek of Revelation is rugged and vivid, but notoriously incorrect. Further, the writer of the Fourth Gospel studiously avoids any mention of his own name; the John of Revelation repeatedly mentions his. Still further, the ideas of the two books are different. The great ideas of the Fourth Gospel – light, life, truth and grace – do not dominate Revelation. At the same time, there are enough resemblances in thought and language to make it clear that both books come from the same centre and from the same world of thought.

The Date of Revelation

We have two sources which enable us to fix the date.

(1) There is the account which tradition gives to us. The consistent tradition is that John was banished to Patmos in

the time of the Roman emperor Domitian, and that he saw his visions there; at the death of Domitian, John was liberated and came back to Ephesus, and there set down the visions he had seen. Victorinus, who wrote towards the end of the third century AD, says in his commentary on Revelation: 'John, when he saw these things, was in the island of Patmos, condemned to the mines by Domitian the emperor. There, therefore, he saw the revelation ... When he was afterwards set free from the mines, he handed down this revelation which he had received from God.' The biblical scholar Jerome, who wrote at the end of the fourth century and the beginning of the fifth, is even more detailed: 'In the fourteenth year after the persecution of Nero, John was banished to the island of Patmos, and there wrote the Revelation ... Upon the death of Domitian, and upon the repeal of his acts by the senate, because of their excessive cruelty, he returned to Ephesus, when Nerva was emperor.' The early Church historian Eusebius says: 'The apostle and evangelist John related these things to the churches, when he had returned from exile in the island after the death of Domitian.' Tradition makes it certain that John saw his visions in exile in Patmos; the only thing that is doubtful – and it is not important – is whether he wrote them down during the time of his banishment or when he returned to Ephesus. On this evidence, we will not be wrong if we date Revelation about AD 95.

(2) The second line of evidence is the material in the book. There is a completely new attitude to Rome and to the Roman Empire.

In Acts, the tribunal of the Roman magistrate was often the safest refuge of the Christian missionaries against the hatred of the Jews and the fury of the mob. Paul was proud that he was a Roman citizen, and he repeatedly claimed the rights to which every Roman citizen was entitled. In Philippi, he put the local magistrates in their place by revealing his citizenship (Acts 16:36–40). In Corinth, Gallio dismissed the complaints against Paul with impartial Roman justice (Acts 18:1–17). In Ephesus, the Roman authorities protected him from the rioting mob (Acts 19:23–41). In Jerusalem, the Roman tribune rescued him from what might have become a lynching (Acts 21:30–40). When the Roman tribune in Jerusalem heard that there was to be an attempt on Paul's life on the way to Caesarea, he took every possible step to ensure Paul's safety (Acts 23:12–31). When Paul despaired of justice in Palestine, he exercised his right as a citizen and appealed direct to Caesar (Acts 25:10–11). When he wrote to the Romans, he urged upon them obedience to the powers that be, because they were ordained by God and were a terror only to the evil and not to the good (Romans 13:1–7). Peter's advice is exactly the same. Governors and kings are to be obeyed, for their task is given to them by God. It is a Christian's duty to fear God and honour the emperor (1 Peter 2:12–17). In writing to the Thessalonians, it is likely that Paul points to the power of Rome as the one thing which is controlling the threatening chaos of the world (2 Thessalonians 2:7).

In Revelation, there is nothing but blazing hatred for Rome. Rome is a Babylon, the mother of prostitutes, drunk with the blood of the saints and the martyrs (Revelation 17:5–6). John hopes for nothing but Rome's total destruction.

The explanation of this change in attitude lies in the wide development of Caesar-worship, which, with its accompanying persecution, is the background of Revelation.

By the time of Revelation, Caesar-worship was the one religion which covered the whole Roman Empire; and it was because of their refusal to conform to its demands that Christians were persecuted and killed. Its essence was that the reigning Roman emperor, who was seen to embody the spirit of Rome, was divine. Once a year, everyone in the Empire had to appear before the magistrates to burn a pinch of incense to the godhead of Caesar and to say: 'Caesar is Lord.' After they had done that, people were able to go away and worship any god or goddess they liked, as long as that worship did not infringe decency and good order; but they had to go through this ceremony in which they acknowledged the emperor's divinity.

The reason was very simple. Rome had a vast and diverse empire, stretching from one end of the known world to the other. It had in it many languages, races and traditions. The problem was how to weld this varied mass into a unity. There was no unifying force such as a common religion, and none of the national religions could conceivably have become universal. Caesar-worship could. It was the one common act and belief which turned the Empire into a unity. To refuse to burn the pinch of incense and to say: 'Caesar is Lord' was not an act against religion; it was an act of political disloyalty. That is why the Romans dealt with the utmost severity with anyone who would not say: 'Caesar is Lord.' And Christians could never give the title Lord to anyone other than Jesus Christ. This was the centre of their creed.

We must see how this Caesar-worship developed and how it was at its peak when Revelation was written.

One basic fact must be noted. Caesar-worship was not imposed on the people from above. It arose from the people; it might even be said that it arose in spite of efforts by the early emperors to stop it, or at least to curb it. And it is to be noted that, of all the people in the Empire, only the Jews were exempt from it.

Caesar-worship began as a spontaneous outburst of gratitude to Rome. The people of the provinces knew very well what they owed to Rome. Impartial Roman justice had taken the place of inconsistent and tyrannical oppression. Security had taken the place of insecurity. The great Roman roads spanned the world, and were safe from robbers; and the seas were clear of pirates. The *pax Romana*, the Roman peace, was the greatest thing which ever happened to the ancient world. As Virgil had it, Rome felt its destiny to be 'to spare the fallen and to cast down the proud'. Life had a new order about it. The American biblical scholar E. J. Goodspeed writes: 'This was the *pax Romana*. The provincial under Roman sway found himself in a position to conduct his business, provide for his family, send his letters, and make his journeys in security, thanks to the strong hand of Rome.'

Caesar-worship did not begin with the deification of the emperor. It began with the deification of Rome. The spirit of the Empire was deified under the name of the goddess Roma. Roma stood for all the strong and benevolent power of the Empire. The first temple to Roma was erected in Smyrna as far back as 195 BC. It was no great step to think of the spirit of Rome as being incarnated in one man, the emperor. The worship of the emperor began with the worship of Julius Caesar after his death. In 29 BC, the Emperor Augustus granted to the provinces of Asia and Bithynia permission to erect temples in Ephesus and Nicaea for the joint worship of the goddess Roma and the deified Julius Caesar. At these shrines, Roman citizens were encouraged and even exhorted to worship. Then another step was taken. To provincials who were *not* Roman citizens, Augustus gave permission to erect temples in Pergamum in Asia and in Nicomedia in Bithynia, for the worship of Roma and *himself*. At first, the worship of the reigning emperor was considered to be something permissible for provincial non-citizens, but not for those who had the dignity of the citizenship.

There was an inevitable development. It is human to worship a god who can be seen rather than a spirit. Gradually, people began more and more to worship the emperor himself instead of the goddess Roma. It still required special permission from the senate to build a temple to the living emperor; but, by the middle of the first century, that permission was more and more freely given. Caesar-worship was becoming the universal religion of the Roman Empire. A priesthood developed, and the worship was organized into groups of ministers and elders called presbyteries, whose officials were held in the highest honour.

This worship was never intended to wipe out other religions. Rome was essentially tolerant. People might worship Caesar *and* their own god. But, more and more, Caesar-worship became a test of political loyalty; it became, as has been said, the recognition of the dominion of Caesar over an individual's life and soul. Let us, then, trace the development of this worship up to, and immediately beyond, the writing of Revelation.

(1) Augustus, who died in AD 14, allowed the worship of Julius Caesar, his great predecessor. He allowed non-citizens in the provinces to worship himself, but he did not permit citizens to do so; and he made no attempt to enforce this worship.

(2) Tiberius (AD 14–37) could not halt Caesar-worship. He forbade temples to be built and priests to be appointed for his own worship; and, in a letter to Gython, a Laconian city, he definitely refused divine honours for himself. So, far from enforcing Caesar-worship, he actively discouraged it.

(3) Caligula (AD 37–41), the next emperor, was an epileptic, a madman and a megalomaniac. He insisted on divine honours. He attempted to enforce Caesar-worship even on the Jews, who had always been and who always were to remain exempt from it. He planned to place his own image in the Holy of Holies in the Temple in Jerusalem, a step which would certainly have provoked unyielding rebellion.

Mercifully, he died before he could carry out his plans. But, in his reign, we have an episode when Caesar-worship became an imperial demand.

(4) Caligula was succeeded by Claudius (AD 41–54), who completely reversed his insane policy. He wrote to the governor of Egypt – there were 1,000,000 Jews in Alexandria – fully approving the Jewish refusal to call the emperor a god and granting them full liberty to enjoy their own worship. On his accession to the throne, he wrote to Alexandria saying: 'I deprecate the appointment of a high priest to me and the erection of temples, for I do not wish to be offensive to my contemporaries, and I hold that sacred fanes [temples] and the like have been by all ages attributed to the immortal gods as peculiar honours.'

(5) Nero (AD 54–68) did not take his own divinity seriously and did nothing to insist on Caesar-worship. It is true that he persecuted the Christians; but this was not because they would not worship him, but because he had to find scapegoats for the great fire of Rome.

(6) On the death of Nero, there were three emperors in eighteen months – Galba, Otho and Vitellius – and in such a time of chaos the question of Caesar-worship did not arise.

(7) The next two emperors, Vespasian (AD 69–79) and Titus (AD 79–81), were wise rulers, who made no insistence on Caesar-worship.

(8) The coming of Domitian (AD 81–96) brought a complete change. He was a devil. He was the worst of all things – a cold-blooded persecutor. With the exception of Caligula, he was the first emperor to take his divinity seriously and to *demand* Caesar-worship. The difference was that Caligula was an insane devil; Domitian was a sane devil, which is much more terrifying. He erected a monument to 'the deified Titus, son of the deified Vespasian'. He began a campaign

of bitter persecution against all who would not worship the ancient gods – 'the atheists', as he called them. In particular, he launched his hatred against the Jews and the Christians. When he arrived in the theatre with his empress, the crowd were urged to rise and shout: 'All hail to our Lord and his Lady!' He behaved as if he himself were a god. He informed all provincial governors that government announcements and proclamations must begin: 'Our Lord and God Domitian commands ...' Everyone who addressed him in speech or in writing must begin: 'Lord and God.'

Here is the background of Revelation. All over the Empire, men and women had to call Domitian god – or die. Caesar-worship was the deliberate policy; all must say: 'Caesar is Lord.' There was no escape.

What were the Christians to do? What hope did they have? Not many of them were wise, and not many of them were powerful. They had no influence or status. Against them had risen the might of Rome, which no nation had ever resisted. They were confronted with the choice – Caesar or Christ. It was to encourage men and women in such times that Revelation was written. John did not shut his eyes to the terrors; he saw dreadful things, and he saw still more dreadful things on the way; but beyond them he saw glory for those who defied Caesar for the love of Christ. Revelation comes from one of the most heroic ages in all the history of the Christian Church. It is true that Domitian's successor Nerva (AD 96–8) repealed the savage laws; but the damage was done, the Christians were outlaws, and Revelation is a clarion call to be faithful to death in order to win the crown of life.

The Book Worth Studying

We cannot shut our eyes to the difficulty of Revelation. It is the most difficult book in the Bible; but its study brings infinite rewards, for it contains the blazing faith of the Christian Church in the days when life was an agony and people expected the end of the heavens and the earth as they knew them but still believed that beyond the terror was the glory and above human raging was the power of God.

REVELATION

GOD'S REVELATION

Revelation 1:1–3

> This is the revelation revealed by Jesus Christ, the
> revelation which God gave to him to show to his servants,
> the revelation which tells of the things which must soon
> happen. This revelation Jesus Christ sent and explained
> through his angel to his servant John, who testified to
> the word sent to him by God and attested by the witness
> borne by Jesus Christ everything which he saw.

THIS book is sometimes called Revelation and sometimes the
Apocalypse. It begins with the words 'The revelation of Jesus
Christ', which mean not the revelation *about* Jesus Christ but
the revelation given *by* Jesus Christ. The Greek word for
revelation is *apokalupsis*, which is a word with a history.

(1) *Apokalupsis* is composed of two parts. *Apo* means *away
from*, and *kalupsis* means a *veiling*. *Apokalupsis*, therefore,
means an *unveiling*, a *revealing*. It was not originally an
especially religious word; it meant simply the disclosure of
any fact. There is an interesting use of it in the writings of the
Greek historian Plutarch (*How to tell a Flatterer from a Friend*,
32). Plutarch tells how Pythagoras once severely rebuked a
devoted disciple of his in public, and the young man went out

and hanged himself. 'From that time on, Pythagoras never admonished anyone when anyone else was present. For error should be treated as a foul disease, and all admonition and *disclosure* [*apokalupsis*] should be in secret.' But *apokalupsis* became especially a Christian word.

(2) It is used for the revealing of God's will to us for our actions. Paul says that he went up to Jerusalem by *apokalupsis*. He went because God told him he wanted him to go (Galatians 2:2).

(3) It is used of the revelation of God's truth to men and women. Paul received his gospel not from a human source but by *apokalupsis* from Jesus Christ (Galatians 1:12). In the Christian assembly, the message of the preacher is an *apokalupsis* (1 Corinthians 14:6).

(4) It is used of God's revealing to men and women of his own mysteries, especially in the incarnation of Jesus Christ (Romans 16:25; Ephesians 3:3).

(5) It is especially used of the revelation of the power and the holiness of God which is to come at the last days. That will be an unveiling of judgment (Romans 2:5); but for Christians it will be an unveiling of praise and glory (1 Peter 1:7), of grace (1 Peter 1:13) and of joy (1 Peter 4:13).

Before we remind ourselves of the more technical use of *apokalupsis*, we may note two things.

(1) This revelation is connected especially with the work of the Holy Spirit (Ephesians 1:17).

(2) We are bound to see that here we have a picture of the whole of the Christian life. There is no part of it which is not lit by the revelation of God. God reveals to us what we must do and say; in Jesus Christ he reveals himself to us, for whoever has seen Jesus has seen the Father (John 14:9); and life moves on to the great and final revelation in which there is judgment for those who have not submitted to God, but there

is grace and glory and joy for those who are in Jesus Christ. Revelation is not a technical theological idea; it is what God is offering to all who will listen.

Now we look at the technical meaning of *apokalupsis*, for that meaning is particularly connected with this book.

The Jews had long since ceased to hope that they would be recognized and upheld as the chosen people by human means. They hoped now for nothing less than the direct intervention of God. To that end, they divided all time into two ages – *this present age*, wholly given over to evil, and *the age to come*, the age of God. Between the two, there was to be a time of terrible trial. Between the Old and the New Testaments, the Jews wrote many books which were visions of the dreadful time before the end and of the blessedness to come. These books were called *Apocalypses*; and that is what Revelation is. Although there is nothing like it in the New Testament, it belongs to a class of literature which was common in the period between the Testaments. All these books are wild and unintelligible, for they are trying to describe the indescribable. The very subject with which Revelation deals is the reason why it is so difficult to understand.

THE MEANS OF GOD'S REVELATION

Revelation 1:1–3 (*contd*)

THIS short section gives us a concise account of how revelation comes to us.

(1) Revelation begins with God, the fountain of all truth. Every truth which we discover is two things – a discovery of the human mind and a gift of God. But it must always be remembered that we never *create* the truth; we *receive* it from God. We must also remember that we can receive it in two

ways. It comes from *earnest seeking*. God gave us minds, and it is often through our minds that he speaks to us. Certainly, he does not grant his truth to those who are too lazy to think. It comes from *reverent waiting*. God sends his truth to those who not only think strenuously but also wait quietly in prayer and in devotion. But it must be remembered that prayer and devotion are not simply passive things. They are the dedicated listening for the voice of God.

(2) God gives this revelation to Jesus Christ. The Bible never, as it were, makes a second God of Jesus; rather, it stresses his utter dependence on God. 'My teaching', said Jesus, 'is not mine but his who sent me' (John 7:16). 'I do nothing on my own, but I speak these things as the Father instructed me' (John 8:28). 'I have not spoken on my own, but the Father who sent me has himself given me a commandment about what to say and what to speak' (John 12:49). It is God's truth that Jesus brings; and that is precisely why his teaching is unique and final.

(3) Jesus sends that truth to John through his angel (Revelation 1:1). Here, the writer of Revelation was a child of his time. At this point in history, people were particularly conscious of the transcendence of God. That is to say, they were impressed above all with the difference between God and the world – so much so that they felt that direct communication between God and human beings was impossible and that there must always be some intermediary. In the Old Testament story, Moses received the law directly from the hands of God (Exodus 19–20); but twice in the New Testament it is said that the law was given by angels (Acts 7:53; Galatians 3:19).

(4) Finally, the revelation is given to John. It is most uplifting to remember the part that individuals play in the coming of God's revelation. God must find someone to

whom he can entrust his truth and whom he can use as his mouthpiece.

(5) Let us note the *content* of the revelation which comes to John. It is the revelation of 'the things which *must soon take place*' (1:1). There are two important words here. There is *must*. History is not haphazard; it has purpose. There is *soon*. Here is the proof that it is quite wrong to use Revelation as a kind of mysterious timetable of what is going to happen thousands of years from now. As John sees it, the things that it deals with are working themselves out immediately. Revelation must be interpreted against the background of its own time.

SERVANTS OF GOD

Revelation 1:1–3 (*contd*)

TWICE, the word *servant* appears in this passage. God's revelation was sent to his *servants*, and it was sent through his *servant* John. In Greek the word is *doulos*, and in Hebrew *ebedh*. Each is difficult to translate fully. The normal translation of *doulos* is *slave*. The real *servant* of God is, in fact, his *slave*. Those who are in service to others can leave their work when they like; they have stated hours of employment and stated hours of freedom; they work for a wage; they have minds of their own and can bargain as to when and for what they will give their labour. Slaves can do none of these things; they are the absolute possessions of their owners, with neither time nor will of their own. *Doulos* and *ebedh* bring out how absolutely we must surrender life to God.

It is of the greatest interest to note to whom these words are applied in Scripture.

Abraham is the servant of God (Genesis 26:24; Psalm 105:26; Daniel 9:11). Jacob is the servant of God (Isaiah

29

44:1–2, 45:4; Ezekiel 37:25). Caleb and Joshua are the servants of God (Numbers 14:24; Joshua 24:29; Judges 2:8; 2 Chronicles 24:6; Nehemiah 1:7, 10:29; Psalm 105:26; Daniel 9:11). David is second only to Moses as characteristically the servant of God (Psalm 132:10, 144:10; 1 Kings 8:66, 11:36; 2 Kings 19:34, 20:6; 1 Chronicles 17:4; in the titles of Psalms 18 and 36; Psalm 89:3; Ezekiel 34:24). Elijah is the servant of God (2 Kings 9:36, 10:10). Isaiah is the servant of God (Isaiah 20:3). Job is the servant of God (Job 1:8, 42:7). The prophets are the servants of God (2 Kings 21:10; Amos 3:7). The apostles are the servants of God (Philippians 1:1; Titus 1:1; James 1:1; Jude 1; Romans 1:1; 2 Corinthians 4:5). A man like Epaphras is the servant of God (Colossians 4:12). All Christians are the servants of God (Ephesians 6:6).

Two things emerge from this.

(1) The greatest people regarded as their greatest honour the fact that they were servants of God.

(2) We must note how wide this service is. Moses, the law-giver; Abraham, the adventurous pilgrim; David, shepherd boy, sweet singer of Israel, king of the nation; Caleb and Joshua, soldiers and men of action; Elijah and Isaiah, prophets and men of God; Job, faithful in misfortune; the apostles, who carried the story of Jesus to others; every Christian – all are *servants of God*. There is not one of us whom God cannot use, if we will submit to his service.

THOSE WHO ARE BLESSED

Revelation 1:1–3 (*contd*)

THIS passage ends with a threefold blessing.

(1) The one who reads these words is blessed. The *reader* here mentioned is not the private reader but the person who

publicly reads the word in the presence of the congregation.
The reading of Scripture was the centre of any Jewish service
(Luke 4:16; Acts 13:15). In the Jewish synagogue, Scripture
was read to the congregation by seven ordinary members of
the congregation, although if a priest or Levite was present
he took precedence. The Christian Church took much of its
service from the synagogue order, and the reading of Scripture
remained a central part of the service. The second-century
writer Justin Martyr gives an account of what a Christian
service was like; and it includes the reading of 'the memoirs
of the apostles [i.e. the gospels], and the writings of the
prophets' (*Apology*, 1:67). *Reader* became in time an official
office in the Church. One of the early Christian theologian
Tertullian's complaints about the heretical sects was the way
in which a person could too speedily arrive at office without
any training for it. He writes: 'And so it comes to pass that
today one man is their bishop, and tomorrow another; today
he is a deacon who tomorrow is a *reader*' (*On Prescription
against Heretics*, 41).

(2) The one who hears these words is blessed. We do well
to remember how great a privilege it is to hear the word of
God in our own language, a privilege which was bought at
great cost. People died to give it to us; and, for a long time,
the professional clergy sought to keep it to themselves. To
this day, the task of giving people the Scriptures in their own
language goes on.

(3) The one who keeps these words is blessed. To hear
God's word is a privilege; to obey it is a duty. There is no real
Christianity in anyone who hears and forgets or deliberately
disregards.

That is all the more true because time is short. The time is
near (verse 3). The early Church lived in vivid expectation of the
coming of Jesus Christ, and that expectation was 'the ground of

hope in distress and constant heed to warning'. Quite apart from that, none of us knows when the call will come to take us from this earth, and in order to meet God with confidence we must add the obedience of our lives to the capacity to listen.

We may note that there are seven *blesseds* in Revelation.

(1) There is the *blessed* we have just studied. We may call it the blessedness of reading, hearing and obeying the word of God.

(2) Blessed are the dead who from now on die in the Lord (14:13). We may call it the blessedness in heaven of Christ's friends on earth.

(3) Blessed is the one who stays awake and is clothed (16:15). We may call it the blessedness of the watchful pilgrim.

(4) Blessed are those who are invited to the marriage supper of the Lamb (19:9). We may call it the blessedness of the invited guests of God.

(5) Blessed and holy are those who share in the first resurrection (20:6). We may call it the blessedness of those whom death cannot touch.

(6) Blessed is the one who keeps the words of the prophecy of this book (22:7). We may call it the blessedness of the wise reader of God's word.

(7) Blessed are those who have washed their robes (22:14). We may call it the blessedness of those who accept the sacrifice of Jesus Christ.

Such blessedness is open to every Christian.

THE MESSAGE AND ITS DESTINATION

Revelation 1:4-6

> This is John writing to the seven churches which are in
> Asia. Grace be to you and peace from him who is and

who was and who is to come, and from the seven spirits
which are before his throne, and from Jesus Christ, the
witness on whom you can rely, the first-born of the dead,
and the ruler of the kings of the earth. To him who loves
us and who set us free from our sins at the cost of his own
blood, and who made us a kingdom, priests to his God and
Father, to him be glory and dominion forever. Amen.

REVELATION is a letter, written to the *seven churches that are
in Asia*. In the New Testament, Asia is never the continent
but always the Roman province. It had been the kingdom
of Attalus III, who had willed it to the Romans at his death.
It included the western sea coast of Asia Minor, on the shores
of the Mediterranean, with Phrygia, Mysia, Caria and Lycia in
the hinterland; and its capital was the city of Pergamum.

The seven churches are named in verse 11 – Ephesus,
Smyrna, Pergamum, Thyatira, Sardis, Philadelphia and
Laodicea. These were by no means the only churches in Asia.
There were churches at Colosse (Colossians 1:2), Hierapolis
(Colossians 4:13), Troas (2 Corinthians 2:12; Acts 20:5),
Miletus (Acts 20:17), Magnesia and Tralles, as the letters of
Ignatius, the Bishop of Antioch, show. Why did John single
out only these seven? There can be more than one reason for
his selection.

(1) These churches might be regarded as the centres of
seven postal districts, being all on a kind of ring road, or
gyratory system, which circled the interior of the province.
Troas was off the beaten track. But Hierapolis and Colosse
were within walking distance of Laodicea; and Tralles,
Magnesia and Miletus were close to Ephesus. Letters delivered
to these seven cities would easily circulate in the surrounding
areas; and, since every letter had to be handwritten, each letter
would need to be sent where it would reach most easily the
greatest number of people.

(2) Any reading of Revelation will show John's preference for the number seven. It occurs fifty-four times. There are seven candlesticks (1:12), seven stars (1:16), seven lamps (4:5), seven seals (5:1), seven horns and seven eyes (5:6), seven thunders (10:3), seven angels, plagues and bowls (15:6–8). The ancient peoples regarded seven as the perfect number, and it runs all through Revelation.

From this, certain of the early commentators drew an interesting conclusion. Seven is the perfect number because it stands for *completeness*. It is, therefore, suggested that, when John wrote to *seven* churches, he was, in fact, writing to the *whole* Church. The first list of New Testament books, called the Muratorian Canon, says of Revelation: 'For John also, though he wrote in the Revelation to seven churches, nevertheless speaks to them all.' This is all the more likely when we remember how often John says: 'Let anyone who has an ear listen to what the Spirit is saying to the churches' (2:7, 2:11, 2:17, 2:29, 3:6, 3:13, 3:22).

(3) Although the reasons we have offered for the choice of these seven churches may be valid, it may be still more valid that John chose them because in them he had a special authority. They were in a special sense *his* churches – and by speaking to them he sent a message first to those who knew and loved him best, and then through them to every church in every generation.

THE BLESSING AND ITS SOURCE

Revelation 1:4–6 (*contd*)

JOHN begins by sending them the blessing of God.

He sends them *grace*, and this means all the undeserved gifts of the wondrous love of God. He sends them *peace*, which

R. H. Charles describes in his commentary as 'the harmony restored between God and man through Christ'. But there are two extraordinary things in this greeting.

(1) John sends blessings from him who is and who was and who is to come. That is in itself a common title for God. In Exodus 3:14, the word of God to Moses is: 'I am who I am.' The Jewish Rabbis explained that by saying that God meant: 'I was; I still am; and in the future I will be.' The Greeks spoke of 'Zeus who was, Zeus who is, and Zeus who will be.' The Orphic worshippers, who followed one of the mystery religions, said: 'Zeus is the first and Zeus is the last; Zeus is the head and Zeus is the middle; and from Zeus all things come.' This is what in Hebrews so beautifully became: 'Jesus Christ is the same yesterday and today and for ever' (Hebrews 13:8).

But, to get the full meaning of this, we must look at it in the Greek, for John breaks free of the rules of grammar to show his reverence for God. We translate the first phrase as *from him who is*; but that is not what the Greek says. A Greek noun is in the nominative case when it is the subject of a sentence, but when it is governed by a preposition it changes its case and *its form*. It is the same in English. *He* is the subject of a sentence; *him* is the object. When John says that the blessing comes *from him who is*, he should have put *him who is* in the genitive case after the preposition; but quite ungrammatically he leaves it in the nominative. It is as if we said in English *from he who is*, refusing to change *he* into *him*. John has such an immense reverence for God that he refuses to alter the form of his name even when the rules of grammar demand it.

John is not finished with his amazing use of language. The second phrase is *from him who was*. Literally, John says *from the he was*. The point is that *who was* would be in Greek a participle. The odd thing is that the verb *eimi* (*to be*) has no past participle. Instead, there is used the participle *genomenos* from the verb *gignomai*, which means not only *to be* but also *to become*. *Becoming* implies change, and John utterly refuses to apply any word to God that will imply any change; and so he uses a Greek phrase that is grammatically impossible and that had never been used before.

In the terrible days in which he was writing, John set his heart on the changelessness of God and used defiance of grammar to underline his faith.

THE SEVENFOLD SPIRIT

Revelation 1:4–6 (*contd*)

ANYONE who reads this passage must be astonished at the form of the Trinity which we meet here. We speak of Father, Son and Holy Spirit. Here, we have God the Father and Jesus Christ the Son – but, instead of the Holy Spirit, we have *the seven Spirits who are before his throne*. These seven Spirits are mentioned more than once in Revelation (3:1, 4:5, 5:6). Three main explanations have been offered of them.

(1) The Jews talked of the seven angels of the presence, whom they beautifully called 'the seven first white ones' (1 Enoch 90:21). They were what we call the archangels who 'stand ready and enter before the glory of the Lord' (Tobit 12:15). Their names are not always the same, but they are often called Uriel, Raphael, Raguel, Michael, Gabriel, Saiquael and Jeremiel. They had the care of the elements of the world – fire, air and water – and were the guardian angels of the nations. They were the most illustrious and the most intimate servants of God. Some think that they are the seven Spirits mentioned here. But that cannot be; great as the angels were, they were still created beings.

(2) The second explanation connects them with the famous passage in Isaiah 11:2. As the Septuagint, the Greek edition of the Hebrew Scriptures that was most widely used in the synagogues in New Testament times, has it: 'The spirit of the Lord shall rest upon him, the spirit of wisdom and understanding, the spirit of counsel and might, the spirit of knowledge and piety; by this spirit he shall be filled with the fear of God.' This passage is the basis of the great concept of *the sevenfold gifts of the Spirit*. As the ninth-century hymn has it:

> Come, Holy Ghost, our souls inspire
> And lighten with celestial fire;
> Thou the anointing Spirit art,
> Who dost thy sevenfold gifts impart.

The Spirit, as the eighth-century Spanish Benedictine, Beatus, said, is one in name but sevenfold in virtues. If we think of the sevenfold gift of the Spirit, it is not difficult to think of the Spirit as seven Spirits, each giving great gifts to men and women. So it is suggested that the idea of the sevenfold gifts of the Spirit gave rise to the image of the seven Spirits before the throne of God.

(3) The third explanation connects the idea of the seven Spirits with the fact of the seven churches. In Hebrews 2:4, we read of God giving 'gifts of the Holy Spirit'. The word translated as *gifts* is *merismos*, and it really means *shares*, as if the idea was that God gives a share of his Spirit to every individual. So, the idea here would be that the seven Spirits stand for the share of the Spirit which God gave to each of the seven churches. It would mean that no Christian fellowship is left without the presence and the power and the illumination of the Spirit.

THE TITLES OF JESUS

Revelation 1:4–6 (*contd*)

In this passage, three great titles are given to Jesus Christ.

(1) He is the witness on whom we can rely. It is a favourite idea of the Fourth Gospel that Jesus is a witness of the truth of God. Jesus said to Nicodemus: 'Very truly, I tell you, we speak of what we know and testify to what we have seen' (John 3:11). Jesus said to Pilate: 'For this I came into the world, to testify to the truth' (John 18:37). A witness is essentially a person who speaks from first-hand knowledge. That is why Jesus is God's witness. He is uniquely the person with first-hand knowledge about God.

(2) He is the first-born of the dead. The word for *first-born* is *prōtotokos*. It can have two meanings. (a) It can mean literally *first-born*. If it is used in this sense, the reference must be to the resurrection. Through his resurrection, Jesus gained a victory over death, which all who believe in him may share. (b) Since the first-born was the son who inherited his father's honour and power, *prōtotokos* comes to mean *one with power and honour, one who occupies the first place*. When Paul speaks of Jesus as the first-born of all creation (Colossians 1:15), he means that the first place of honour and glory belongs to him. If we take the word in this sense – and probably we should – it means that Jesus is Lord of the dead as he is Lord of the living. There is no part of the universe, in this world or in the world to come, and nothing in life or in death of which Jesus Christ is not Lord.

(3) He is the ruler of kings on earth. There are two things to note here. (a) This is a reminiscence of Psalm 89:27: 'I will make him the firstborn, the highest of the kings of the earth.' That was always taken by Jewish scholars to be a description

of the coming Messiah; and, therefore, to say that Jesus is the ruler of kings on earth is to claim that he is the Messiah. (b) In *The Apocalypse of St John*, H. B. Swete very beautifully points out the connection between this title of Jesus and the temptation story. In that story, the devil took Jesus up into a high mountain and showed him all the kingdoms of the earth and their glory and said: 'All these I will give you, if you will fall down and worship me' (Matthew 4:9; Luke 4:6–7). It was the devil's claim that the kingdoms of the earth were delivered into his power (Luke 4:6); and it was his suggestion that, if Jesus would strike a bargain with him, he would give him a share in them. The amazing thing is that what the devil promised Jesus – and could never have given him – Jesus won for himself by the suffering of the cross and the power of the resurrection. Not compromise with evil but the unswerving loyalty and the unfailing love which accepted the cross brought Jesus his universal lordship.

WHAT JESUS DID FOR US

Revelation 1:4–6 (*contd*)

FEW passages set down with such splendour what Jesus did for us.

(1) He loves us, and he set us free from our sins at the cost of his own blood. The Authorized Version is incorrect here. It reads: 'Unto him that loved us and *washed* us from our sins in his own blood.' The words *to wash* and *to set free* are very alike in Greek. *To wash* is *louein*; *to set free* is *luein*; and they are pronounced in exactly the same way. But there is no doubt that the oldest and best Greek manuscripts read *luein*. Again, *in his own blood* is a mistranslation. The word translated as *in* is *en*, which, indeed, can mean *in*; but here it is a translation

of the Hebrew word *be* (the *e* is pronounced very short as in *the*), which means *at the price of*.

What Jesus did, as John sees it, was to free us from our sins at the cost of his own blood. This is exactly what he says later on when he speaks of those who were ransomed for God by the blood of the Lamb (5:9). It is exactly what Paul meant when he spoke of us being *redeemed* from the curse of the law (Galatians 3:13) and when he spoke of *redeeming* those who were under the law (Galatians 4:5). In both cases, the word used is *exagorazein*, which means *to buy out from*, to pay the price of buying a person or a thing out of the possession of the one who holds power over that person or thing.

This is a very interesting and important correction of the Authorized Version. It is made in all the newer translations, and it means that the well-worn phrases which speak of being 'washed in the blood of the Lamb' have little scriptural authority. These phrases convey a staggering picture; and it must come to many with a certain relief to know that what John said was that we are set free from our sins at the cost of the blood, that is, at the cost of the life of Jesus Christ.

There is another very significant thing here. We must note carefully the tenses of the verbs. John says that Jesus *loves* us and *set us free*. *Loves* is the *present tense*, and it means that the love of God in Christ Jesus is something which is continuous. *Set us free* is the *past tense*, the Greek aorist, which tells of one act completed in the past – and it means that in the one act of the cross our liberation from sin was achieved. That is to say, what happened on the cross was one act in time which was for our benefit and an expression of the continuous love of God.

(2) Jesus made us a kingdom, priests to God. That is a quotation of Exodus 19:6: 'You shall be for me a priestly kingdom and a holy nation.' Jesus has done two things for us.

(a) He has given us royalty. Through him we may become the true children of God; and, if we are children of the King of Kings, we are part of the most royal ancestry of all.

(b) He made us priests. The point is this. Under the old way, only the priest had the right of access to God. When the Jews entered the Temple, they could pass through the Court of the Gentiles, the Court of the Women and the Court of the Israelites – but there they must stop; into the Court of the Priests they could not go; they could come no nearer the Holy of Holies. In the vision of the great days to come, Isaiah said: 'You shall be called priests of the Lord' (Isaiah 61:6). In that day, every one of the people would be a priest and have access to God. That is what John means; because of what Jesus Christ did, access to the presence of God is now open to everyone. There is a priesthood of all believers. We can come boldly to the throne of grace (Hebrews 4:16), because for us there is a new and living way into the presence of God (Hebrews 10:19–22).

THE COMING GLORY

Revelation 1:7

> Behold, he is coming with the clouds, and every eye
> shall see him, and the people who pierced him will see
> him; and all the tribes of the earth shall lament over him.
> Yea! Amen!

FROM now on in almost every passage, we shall have to note John's repeated use of the Old Testament. He was so familiar with the Old Testament and it was so much a part of his thinking that it was almost impossible for him to write a paragraph without quoting it. This is interesting and significant. John was living in a time when to be a Christian was desperately difficult. He himself had experienced banishment and imprisonment and hard labour; and there were many who met their deaths in the most cruel ways. The best way to maintain courage and hope in such a situation was to remember that God had never failed in the past and that his power had not grown less now.

In this passage, John sets down the motto and the text of his whole book, his confidence in the triumphant return of Christ, which would rescue Christians in distress from the cruelty of their enemies.

(1) To Christians, the return of Christ is a *promise on which to feed the soul*. John takes as his picture of that return Daniel's vision of the four great beasts, the powers which have held the world in their grip (Daniel 7:1–14). There was Babylon, the power that was like a lion with eagle's wings (7:4). There was Persia, the power that was like a savage bear (7:5). There was Greece, the power that was like a winged leopard (7:6). There was Rome, a beast with iron teeth, beyond description (7:7). But the day of these bestial empires was over, and the dominion was to be given to a gentle power like a son of man. 'As I watched in the night visions, I saw one like a [son of man] coming with the clouds of heaven. And he came to the Ancient One and was presented before him. To him was given dominion and glory and kingship, that all peoples, nations and languages should serve him' (7:13–14). It is from that passage in Daniel that there emerges the ever-recurring picture of the Son of Man coming on the clouds (Mark 13:26, 14:62; Matthew 24:30, 26:64). When we strip away the purely temporary imagery – we, for instance, no longer think of heaven as a localized place above the sky – we are left with the unchanging truth that the day will come when Jesus Christ will be Lord of all. In that hope, there has always been the source of strength and the comfort of Christians for whom life was difficult and for whom faith meant death.

(2) To the enemies of Christ, *the return of Christ is a threat*. To make this point, John again quotes the Old Testament, from Zechariah 12:10, which contains the words: 'When they look on the one whom they have pierced, they shall mourn for him, as one mourns for an only child, and weep bitterly over him, as one weeps over a firstborn.' The story behind the Zechariah saying is this. God gave his people a good shepherd; but the people in their disobedient folly killed him and took to themselves evil and self-seeking shepherds. But the day will come when in the grace of God they will bitterly repent, and in that day they will look on the good shepherd whom they pierced and will sorrowfully lament for him and for what they have done. John takes that picture and applies it to Jesus. The day will come when all people, even those who crucified him, will look on him again; and, this time, he will be not a broken figure on a cross but a regal figure to whom universal dominion has been given.

The first reference of these words is to the Jews and the Romans who actually crucified Jesus. But, in every age, all who sin crucify him again. The day will come when those who disregarded and those who opposed Jesus Christ will find him the Lord of the universe and the judge of their souls.

The passage closes with the two exclamations: 'Even so. Amen!' In the Greek, the words are *nai* and *amēn*. *Nai* is the Greek and *amēn* is the Hebrew for a solemn affirmation – 'Yes, indeed! So let it be!' By using the expression in both Greek and Hebrew, John underlines its fearful solemnity.

THE GOD IN WHOM WE TRUST

Revelation 1:8

> I am alpha and omega, says the Lord God, he who is and
> who was and who is to come, the Almighty.

HERE is a tremendous description of the God in whom we trust and whom we adore.

(1) He is alpha and omega. *Alpha* is the first letter and *omega* the last of the Greek alphabet; and the phrase *alpha to omega* indicates completeness. The first letter of the Hebrew alphabet is *aleph* and the last is *tau*; and the Jews used the same kind of expression. The Rabbis said that Adam broke the law and Abraham kept it from *aleph* to *tau*. They said that God had blessed Israel from *aleph* to *tau*. This expression indicates that God is absolutely complete: he has in himself what the biblical scholar H. B. Swete called 'the boundless life which embraces all and transcends all'.

(2) God is he who is and who was and who is to come. That is to say, he is the Eternal. He was before time began; he is now; and he will be when time ends. He has been the God of all who have trusted in him; he is the God in whom at this present moment we can put our trust; and there can be no event and no time in the future which can separate us from him. As the Scottish Paraphrase has it:

> Nor death nor life, nor earth nor hell,
>   nor time's destroying sway,
> Can e'er efface us from his heart,
>   or make his love decay.
>
> Each future period that will bless,
>   as it has bless'd the past;
> He lov'd us from the first of time,
>   He loves us to the last.

(3) God is the Almighty. The word for *Almighty* is *pantokratōr*, which describes the one who has dominion over all things.

The significant fact is that this word occurs in the New Testament seven times. It occurs once in 2 Corinthians 6:18,

44

in a quotation from the Old Testament; and the remaining six instances are all in Revelation. This word is characteristic of John. Think of the circumstances in which he was writing. The embattled might of Rome had risen up to crush the Christian Church. No empire had ever been able to withstand Rome; what possible chance against Rome had those whom the English poet Sir William Watson described as 'the panting, huddled flock whose crime was Christ'? Humanly speaking, the Christian Church had no chance at all; but, if people thought that, they had left the most important factor of all out of the reckoning – God the *pantokratōr*, in the grip of whose hand were all things.

It is this word which in the Greek Old Testament describes 'the Lord of Sabbaoth, the Lord of hosts' (Amos 9:5; Hosea 12:5). It is this word which John uses in the tremendous text: 'The Lord our God the Almighty reigns' (Revelation 19:6). If we are in the hands of a God like that, nothing can pluck us away. If behind the Christian Church there is a God like that, as long as the Church is true to its Lord, nothing can destroy it. As William Freeman Lloyd's hymn has it:

> My times are in thy hand:
>   I'll always trust in thee;
> And, after death, at thy right hand
>   I shall for ever be.

THROUGH TRIBULATION TO THE KINGDOM

Revelation 1:9

I, John, your brother and partner in tribulation, in the kingdom, and in that steadfast endurance which life in Christ alone can give, was in the island which is called

> Patmos, for the sake of the word given by God and
> confirmed by Jesus Christ.

JOHN introduces himself, not by any official title but as *your brother and partner in tribulation*. His right to speak was that he had come through all that those to whom he was writing were going through. Ezekiel writes in his book: 'I came to the exiles at Tel-abib, who lived by the river Chebar. And I sat there among them, stunned' (Ezekiel 3:5). People will never listen to anyone who preaches endurance from the comfort of an easy chair, nor to someone who preaches heroic courage to others from a position of prudent safety. It is the person who has already experienced the time of trouble who can help others who are going through it. As the native Americans have it: 'No man can criticize another man until he has walked for a day in his moccasins.' John and Ezekiel could speak because they had sat where their people were sitting.

John puts three words together – tribulation, kingdom and steadfast endurance. *Tribulation* is *thlipsis*. Originally, *thlipsis* meant simply *pressure* and could, for instance, describe the pressure of a great stone on someone's body. At first it was used quite literally, but in the New Testament it has come to describe the pressure of events which constitutes persecution. *Steadfast endurance* is *hupomonē*. *Hupomonē* does not describe the patience which simply passively submits to the tide of events; it describes the spirit of courage and conquest which leads to gallantry and transforms even suffering into glory. The situation of the Christians was this. They were in *thlipsis* and, as John saw it, in the midst of the terrible events which preceded the end of the world. They were looking towards *basileia*, the kingdom, into which they desired to enter and on which they had set their hearts. There was only one way from *thlipsis* to *basileia*, from affliction to glory, and that was through *hupomonē*, conquering endurance. Jesus said: 'Anyone who endures to the end will be saved' (Matthew 24:13). Paul told his people: 'It is through many persecutions that we must enter the kingdom of God' (Acts 14:22). In 2 Timothy, we read: 'If we endure, we will also reign with him' (2 Timothy 2:12).

The way to the kingdom is the way of endurance. But, before we leave this passage, we must note one thing. That endurance is to be found in Christ. He himself endured to the end, and he can enable those who walk with him to achieve the same endurance and to reach the same goal.

THE ISLAND OF BANISHMENT

Revelation 1:9 (*contd*)

JOHN tells us that, when the visions of Revelation came to him, he was in Patmos. It was the unanimous tradition of the early Church that he was banished to Patmos in the reign of Domitian. Jerome says that John was banished in the fourteenth year after Nero and liberated on the death of Domitian (*Concerning Illustrious Men*, 9). This would mean that he was banished to Patmos in about AD 94 and liberated in about AD 96.

Patmos, a barren, rocky little island belonging to a group of islands called the Sporades, is ten miles long by five miles wide. It is crescent-shaped, with the horns of the crescent pointing to the east. Its shape makes it a good natural harbour. It lies forty miles off the coast of Asia Minor, and it was important because it was the last haven on the voyage from Rome to Ephesus and the first in the reverse direction.

Banishment to a remote island was a common form of Roman punishment. It was a punishment usually handed out to political prisoners – and, as far as they were concerned, there were worse alternatives. Such banishment involved the loss of civil rights and all property except enough for a bare existence. People banished in this way were not personally ill-treated and were not confined in prison on their island but were free to move within its narrow limits. Such would be banishment for a political prisoner; but it would be very different for John. He was a leader of the Christians, and Christians were criminals. The wonder is that he was not executed straightaway. Banishment for him would involve hard labour in the quarries. The archaeologist and New Testament scholar Sir William Ramsay says that his banishment would be 'preceded by scourging, marked by perpetual fetters, scanty clothing, insufficient food, sleep on the bare ground, a dark prison, work under the lash of the military overseer'.

Patmos left its mark on John's writing. To this day, visitors are shown a cave in a cliff overlooking the sea, where it is said that Revelation was written. There are magnificent views of the sea from Patmos; and, as the commentator James Strahan says, Revelation is full of 'the sights and the sounds of the infinite sea'. The word *thalassa*, sea, occurs in Revelation no fewer than twenty-five times. Strahan writes: 'Nowhere is "the voice of many waters" more musical than in Patmos; nowhere does the rising and setting sun make a more splendid "sea of glass mingled with fire"; yet nowhere is the longing more natural that the separating sea should be no more.'

It was to all the hardships and pain and weariness of banishment and hard labour on Patmos that John went *for the sake of the word given by God*. As far as the Greek goes, that phrase is capable of three interpretations. It could mean that John went to Patmos to *preach* the word of God. It could mean that he withdrew to the loneliness of Patmos to *receive* the word of God and the visions of Revelation. But it is quite

certain that it means that it was John's unshakable loyalty to the
word of God, and his insistence on preaching the message of
Jesus Christ, which brought him to banishment in Patmos.

IN THE SPIRIT ON THE LORD'S DAY

Revelation 1:10–11

> I was in the Spirit on the Lord's Day, and I heard behind
> me a great voice, like the sound of a trumpet, saying:
> 'Write what you see in a book, and send it to the seven
> churches, to Ephesus and to Smyrna, and to Pergamos
> and to Thyatira and to Sardis and to Philadelphia and to
> Laodicea.'

HISTORICALLY this is an extremely interesting passage, for it
is the first reference in literature to the Lord's Day.

We have often spoken of the day of the Lord, that day of
wrath and judgment when this present age with all its evil was
to be shatteringly changed into the age to come. Some think
that John is saying that he was transported in a vision to that
day of the Lord and saw in advance all the astonishing things
which were to happen then. Those who hold that view are very
few, and it is not a natural meaning for the words.

It is quite certain that when John uses the expression *the
Lord's Day* he is using it as we use it – its very first mention
in literature.

How did the Christian Church cease to observe the Sabbath,
Saturday, and come to observe the Lord's Day, Sunday? The
Sabbath commemorated God's rest after the creation of the
world; the Lord's Day commemorates the rising of Jesus from
the dead.

The three earliest references to the Lord's Day may well
be the following. The *Didache*, the Teaching of the Twelve

Apostles, the first manual of Christian worship and instruction, says of the Christian Church: 'On the Lord's Day we meet and break bread' (*Didache*, 14:1). Ignatius of Antioch, writing to the Magnesians, describes the Christians as 'no longer living for the Sabbath, but for the Lord's Day' (*To the Magnesians*, 9:1). The second-century Christian writer Melito of Sardis wrote a treatise *Concerning the Lord's Day*. By early in the second century, the Sabbath had been abandoned and the Lord's Day was the accepted Christian day.

One thing seems certain. All these early references come from Asia Minor, and it was there that the observance of the Lord's Day first came in. But what was it that suggested to the Christians a *weekly* observance of the first day of the week? In the middle east, there was a day of the month and a day of the week called *Sebastē*, which means *the Emperor's Day*; it was no doubt this which made the Christians decide that the first day of the week must be dedicated to their Lord.

John was *in the Spirit*. This phrase means that he was in an ecstasy in which he was lifted beyond the things of space and time into the world of eternity. 'The spirit lifted me up,' said Ezekiel (Ezekiel 3:12), 'and ... I heard behind me the sound of loud rumbling.' For John, the voice was like the sound of a trumpet. The sound of the trumpet is woven into the language of the New Testament (Matthew 24:31; 1 Corinthians 15:52; 1 Thessalonians 4:16). There is no doubt that in the mind of John there is here another Old Testament picture. In the account of the giving of the law, it is said: 'There was thunder and lightning, as well as a thick cloud on the mountain, and a blast of a trumpet' (Exodus 19:16). The voice of God sounds with the commanding, unmistakable clarity of a trumpet-call.

John is told to write the vision that he sees. It is his duty to share the message which God gives to him. There is an obligation first to hear and then to transmit, even if the price of the transmission is indeed costly. It may be that it is necessary to withdraw to see the vision; but there is also a necessity to go forth to tell it.

Two phrases go together. John was *in Patmos*; and John was *in the Spirit*. We have seen what Patmos was like, and we have seen the pain and the hardship that John was undergoing. No matter where we are, no matter how hard our lives are, no matter what we are passing through, it is still possible to be in the Spirit. And, if John was in the Spirit, even on Patmos, the glory and the message of God still came to him.

THE DIVINE MESSENGER

Revelation 1:12–13

> And I turned to see the voice that was speaking to me; and, when I had turned, I saw seven golden lampstands, and, in the midst of the lampstands, one like a son of man, clothed in a robe that reached to his feet, and girt about the breasts with a golden girdle.

WE now begin on the first of John's visions; and we shall see that he is so familiar with Scripture that element after element in the picture has an Old Testament background and counterpart.

He says that he turned *to see the voice*. We would say: 'I turned to see whose voice it was that was speaking to me.'

When he turned, he saw *seven golden lampstands*. John does not only allude to the Old Testament; he takes items from many places in it, and out of them he forms a composite picture. The picture of the seven golden lampstands has three sources.

(1) It comes from the picture of the candlestick of pure gold in the tabernacle. It was to have six branches, three on one side and three on the other, and seven lamps to give light (Exodus 25:31–7).

(2) It comes from the picture of Solomon's Temple. In it, there were to be five candlesticks of pure gold on the right hand and five on the left (1 Kings 7:49).

(3) It comes from the vision of Zechariah. Zechariah saw 'a lampstand all of gold, with a bowl on the top of it; there are seven lamps on it' (Zechariah 4:2).

When John sees a vision, he sees it in terms of scenes from the Old Testament places and occasions when God had already revealed himself to his people. Surely there is a lesson here. The best way to prepare oneself for new revelation of truth is to study the revelation which God has already given.

In the midst of the lampstands, he saw one *like a son of man*. Here, we are back to the picture of Daniel 7:13, in which the kingdom and the power and the dominion are given by the Ancient One to one like a son of man. As we well know from Jesus' use of it, *Son of Man* became nothing less than the title of the Messiah; and, by using it here, John makes it plain that the revelation which he is to receive is coming from Jesus Christ himself.

This figure was clothed with *a robe which reached down to his feet*, and he was *girt about the breasts with a golden girdle*. Here again we have three pictures.

(1) The word which describes the robe is *podērēs*, *reaching down to the feet*. This is the word which the Greek Old Testament uses to describe the robe of the high priest (Exodus 28:4, 29:5; Leviticus 16:4). The Jewish historian Josephus also describes carefully the garments which the priests and the high priest wore when they were serving in the Temple. They wore 'a long robe reaching to the feet', and, around the

breast, 'higher than the elbows', they wore a girdle which was loosely wound round and round the body. The girdle was embroidered with colours and flowers, with a mixture of gold interwoven (*The Antiquities of the Jews*, 3:7:2, 4). All this means that the description of the robe and the girdle of the glorified Christ is almost exactly that of the clothes of the priests and of the high priest. Here, then, is the symbol of the high priestly character of the work of the risen Lord. A priest, as the Jews saw it, was a man who himself has access to God and who opens the way for others to come to him; even in the heavenly places, Jesus, the great high priest, is still carrying on his priestly work, opening the way for all to the presence of God.

(2) But other people besides priests wore the long robe reaching to the feet and the high girdle. It was the dress of great ones, of princes and of kings. *Podērēs* is the description of the robe of Jonathan (1 Samuel 18:4), of Saul (1 Samuel 24:5, 24:11) and of the princes of the sea (Ezekiel 26:16). The robe the risen Christ was wearing was the robe of royalty. He was no longer a criminal on a cross; he was dressed like a king.

Christ is Priest and Christ is King.

(3) There is still another part of this picture. In the vision of Daniel, the divine figure who came to tell him the truth of God was clothed in fine linen (the Greek Old Testament calls his garment *podērēs*) and with a belt of fine gold (Daniel 10:5). This, then, is the form of dress of the messenger of God. So this presents Jesus Christ as the supreme messenger of God.

Here is a tremendous picture. When we trace the origins of the thought of John, we see that by the very form of dress of the risen Lord he is showing him to us in his threefold eternal office of Prophet, Priest and King, the one who brings the truth of God, the one who enables others to enter into the presence of God and the one to whom God has given the power and dominion forever.

THE PICTURE OF THE RISEN CHRIST

Revelation 1:14–19

> His head and his hair were white, as white wool, like snow; and his eyes were as a flame of fire; and his feet were like beaten brass, as if it had been refined in a furnace; and his voice was as the voice of many waters; he had seven stars in his right hand; and out of his mouth there was coming a sharp two-edged sword; and his face was as the sun shining in its strength. And when I saw him, I fell at his feet like a dead man. And he put his right hand on me and said: 'Stop being afraid. I am the first and the last; I am the living one although I was dead, and, behold, I am alive forever and ever; and I have the keys of death and of Hades. Write down what you have seen, what is and what will be hereafter.'

BEFORE we begin to look at this passage in detail, there are two general facts we must note.

(1) It is easy to miss seeing how carefully constructed Revelation is. It is not a book which was flung together in a hurry; it is a closely integrated and artistic literary whole. In this passage, we have a whole series of descriptions of the risen Christ; and the interesting thing is that each of the letters to the seven churches which follow in the next two chapters, with the exception of the letter to Laodicea, opens with a description of the risen Christ taken from this chapter. It is as if this chapter introduced a series of themes which were later to become the texts for the letters to the churches. Let us set down the beginning of each of the first

six letters and see how it corresponds to the description of the risen Christ here.

> To the angel of the church in Ephesus, write: The words of him *who holds the seven stars in his right hand* (2:1).
>
> To the angel of the church in Smyrna, write: The words of *the first and the last, who was dead and came to life* (2:8).
>
> To the angel of the church in Pergamum, write: The words of him *who has the sharp two-edged sword* (2:12).
>
> To the angel of the church in Thyatira, write: The words of the Son of God, *who has eyes like a flame of fire, and whose feet are like burnished bronze* (2:18).
>
> To the angel of the church in Sardis, write: The words of him *who has* the seven spirits of God and *the seven stars* (3:1).
>
> To the angel of the church in Philadelphia, write: The words of the holy one, the true one, *who has the key of David*, who opens and no one will shut, who shuts and no one opens (3:7).

This is literary craftsmanship of a very high standard.

(2) The second thing to note is that, in this passage, John takes titles which in the Old Testament are descriptions of God and applies them to the risen Christ.

> *His head and his hair were white, as white wool, like snow.*

In Daniel 7:9, that is a description of the Ancient One.

> *His voice was as the sound of many waters.*

In Ezekiel 43:2, that is a description of God's own voice.

He had the seven stars in his hand.

In the Old Testament, it is God himself who controls the stars. It is God's question to Job: 'Can you bind the chains of the Pleiades, or loose the cords of Orion?' (Job 38:31).

I am the first and the last.

Isaiah hears the voice of God saying: 'I am the first and I am the last; besides me there is no god' (Isaiah 44:6; cf. 48:12).

I am the living one.

In the Old Testament, God is characteristically 'the living God' (Joshua 3:10; Psalm 42:2; Hosea 1:10).

I have the keys of death and of Hades.

The Rabbis had a saying that there were three keys which belonged to God and which he would share with no other – the keys of birth, rain and raising the dead.

Nothing could better show the reverence in which John holds Jesus Christ. He holds him so high that he can give him nothing less than the titles which in the Old Testament belong to God. In the words from Thomas Kelly's hymn, 'The Head that Once was Crowned with Thorns':

> The highest place that heaven affords
>   Is his, is his by right,
> The King of kings, and Lord of lords,
>   And heaven's eternal Light.

THE TITLES OF THE RISEN LORD (1)

Revelation 1:14–19 (*contd*)

LET us look very briefly at each of the titles by which the risen Lord is called here.

His head and his hair were white, as white wool, like snow.

This, taken from the description of the Ancient One in Daniel 7:9, is symbolic of two things. (1) It stands for great age; and it speaks to us of the eternal existence of Jesus Christ. (2) It speaks to us of divine purity. The snow and the white wool are the emblems of stainless purity. 'Though your sins are like scarlet,' said Isaiah, 'they shall be like snow; though they are red like crimson, they shall become like wool' (Isaiah 1:18). Here we have the symbols of the pre-existence and the sinlessness of Christ.

His eyes were as a flame of fire.

Daniel is always in John's mind, and this is part of the description of the divine figure who brought the vision to Daniel. 'His eyes like flaming torches' (Daniel 10:6). When we read the gospel story, we get the impression that those who had once seen the eyes of Jesus could never forget them. Again and again, we have the vivid picture of his eyes sweeping round a circle of people (Mark 3:34, 10:23, 11:11); sometimes his eyes flashed in anger (Mark 3:5); sometimes they fastened on someone in love (Mark 10:21); and sometimes they had in them all the sorrow of someone whose friends had wounded him deeply (Luke 22:61).

His feet were like beaten brass, as if it had been refined by fire in a furnace.

The word translated as *beaten brass* is *chalkolibanos*. No one really knows what the metal is. Perhaps it was that fabled compound called *electrum*, which the ancients believed to be an alloy of gold and silver and more precious than either. Here again, it is the Old Testament which gives John his vision.

In Daniel, it is said of the divine messenger that 'his arms and legs [were] like the gleam of burnished bronze' (Daniel 10:6); in Ezekiel, it is said of the angelic beings that their feet 'sparkled like burnished bronze' (Ezekiel 1:7). It may be that we are to see two things in the picture. The brass stands for *strength*, for the steadfastness of God; and the shining rays stand for *speed*, for the swiftness of the feet of God to help his own or to punish sin.

His voice was as the sound of many waters.

This is the description of the voice of God in Ezekiel 43:2. But it may be that we can catch an echo of the little island of Patmos. As H. B. Swete has it in his book *The Apocalypse of John*: 'The roar of the Aegean was in the ears of the seer.' Swete goes on to say that the voice of God is not confined to one note. Here, it is like the thunder of the sea; but it can also be like a still small voice (1 Kings 19:12) or, as the Greek version of the Old Testament has it, like a gentle breeze. It can thunder a rebuke; and it can sing softly with the soothing comfort of a mother over her hurt child.

He had seven stars in his right hand.

Here again, we have something which was the prerogative of God alone. But there is also something lovely. When the seer fell in awed terror before the vision of the risen Christ, the Christ stretched out his right hand and placed it on him and told him not to be afraid. The hand of Christ is strong enough to uphold the heavens and gentle enough to wipe away our tears.

THE TITLES OF THE RISEN LORD (2)

Revelation 1:14-19 (contd)

*There was coming forth from his mouth a sharp,
two-edged sword.*

THE sword referred to was not long and narrow like a fencer's
blade; it was a short, tongue-shaped sword for close fighting.
Again, the seer has searched the Old Testament for his picture.
Isaiah says of God: 'He shall strike the earth with the rod of
his mouth' (Isaiah 11:4); and of himself: 'He made my mouth
like a sharp sword' (Isaiah 49:2). The symbolism tells us of
the penetrating quality of the word of God. If we listen to it,
no shield of self-deception can withstand it; it strips away our
self-deludings, lays bare our sin and leads to pardon. 'The
word of God is living and active, sharper than any two-edged
sword' (Hebrews 4:12). 'And then the lawless one will be
revealed, whom the Lord Jesus will destroy with the breath
of his mouth' (2 Thessalonians 2:8).

His face was as the sun shining in its strength.

In Judges, there is a great picture which may well have been in
John's mind. The enemies of God shall perish, 'But may your
friends be like the sun as it rises in its might' (Judges 5:31).
If that is true of those who love God, how much truer it must
be of God's beloved Son. Swete sees something even lovelier
here – nothing less than a memory of the transfiguration. On
that occasion, Jesus was transfigured before Peter, James and
John, 'and his face shone like the sun' (Matthew 17:2). No one
who had seen that sight could ever forget the glow; and, if the
writer of this book is that same John, perhaps he saw again on
the face of the risen Christ the glory he had glimpsed on the
Mount of Transfiguration.

When I saw him, I fell at his feet like a dead man.

This was the experience of Ezekiel when God spoke to him (Ezekiel 1:28, 3:23, 43:3). But surely we can again find a memory of the gospel story. On that day in Galilee, when there was the great catch of fish and Peter glimpsed who Jesus was, he fell to his knees, conscious only that he was a sinful man (Luke 5:1–11). To the end of the day, there can be nothing but reverence in the presence of the holiness and the glory of the risen Christ.

Stop being afraid.

Surely here, too, we have a reminiscence of the gospel story, for these were words which the disciples had heard more than once from the lips of Jesus. It was in this way that he spoke to them when he came to them across the water (Matthew 14:27; Mark 6:50); and it was above all in this way that he spoke to them on the Mount of Transfiguration, when they were terrified at the sound of the divine voice (Matthew 17:7). Even in heaven, when we come near the unapproachable glory, Jesus is saying: 'I am here; do not be afraid.'

I am the first and the last.

In the Old Testament, this is nothing other than the self-description of God (Isaiah 44:6, 48:12). It is the promise of Jesus that he is there at the beginning and the end. He is there in the moment of birth and at the time of death. He is there when we set out upon the Christian way and when we finish our course. As F. W. H. Myers, in his poem 'Saint Paul', makes Paul say:

> Yea thro' life, death, thro' sorrow and thro' sinning
> He shall suffice me, for he hath sufficed:
> Christ is the end, for Christ was the beginning,
> Christ the beginning, for the end is Christ.

I am the living one, although I was dead and I am alive
forever and forever.

Here is at once the claim and the promise of Christ, the claim
of one who conquered death and the promise of one who is
alive for evermore to be with his people.

I have the keys of death and Hades.

Death has its gates (Psalm 9:13, 107:18; Isaiah 38:10); and
Christ has the keys of these gates. There were those who took
this claim – and some still do – as a reference to the descent
into hell (1 Peter 3:18–20). There was a belief in the ancient
Church that, when Jesus descended into Hades, he unlocked
the doors and brought out Abraham and all God's faithful
people who had lived and died in the generations before.
But we may take it in an even wider sense; for we who
are Christians believe that Jesus Christ has abolished death
and brought life and immortality to light through the gospel
(2 Timothy 1:10), that because he lives we too shall live (John
14:19), and that, therefore, for us and for those whom we love,
the bitterness of death is forever past.

THE CHURCHES AND THEIR ANGELS

Revelation 1:20

Here is the secret meaning of the seven stars which you
saw in my right hand and the seven golden lampstands.
The seven stars are the angels of the seven churches and
the seven lampstands are the seven churches.

THIS passage begins with a word which throughout the New
Testament is used in a very special way. The Authorized
Version speaks of the *mystery* of the seven stars and of the

seven golden candlesticks. The Greek, *mustērion*, does not mean a *mystery* in our sense of the term. It means something which is meaningless to the outsider but meaningful to the initiate who possesses the key. So, here the risen Christ goes on to give the inner meaning of the seven stars and the seven lampstands.

The seven lampstands stand for the seven churches. One of the great titles of Christians is that they are the light of the world (Matthew 5:14; Philippians 2:15). But one of the ancient Greek commentators has a penetrating comment on this. He says that the churches are called not the light itself but the lampstand on which the light is set. It is not the churches themselves which produce the light; the giver of light is Jesus Christ; and the churches are only the vessels within which the light shines. The light which Christians possess is always a borrowed light.

One of the great problems of Revelation is to decide what John means by the *angels of the churches*. More than one explanation has been offered.

(1) The word *aggelos* – *gg* in Greek is pronounced *ng* – has two meanings. It means an *angel*, but more often it means a *messenger*. It is suggested that messengers of all the churches have assembled to receive a message from John and take it back to their congregations. If that is so, each letter will begin: 'To the messenger of the church of ...' As far as the Greek goes, this is perfectly possible, and it gives good sense; but the difficulty is that *aggelos* is used in Revelation about fifty times apart from its use here and in the letters to the seven churches, and without exception it means *angel*.

(2) It is suggested that *aggelos* means a bishop of the churches. It is suggested either that the bishops of the churches have gathered to meet John or that he is directing these letters to them. In favour of this theory, the words of Malachi are

often quoted: 'The lips of a priest should guard knowledge, and people should seek instruction from his mouth, for he is the *messenger* of the Lord of hosts' (Malachi 2:7). In the Septuagint, *messenger* is *aggelos*; and it is suggested that the title could very easily be transferred to the bishops of the churches. They are the messengers of the Lord to their churches, and to them John speaks. Again, this explanation makes good sense; but it suffers from the same objection as the first. It attaches *aggelos* to a human person – and John never does that anywhere else.

(3) It is suggested that this has to do with the idea of guardian angels. In Hebrew thought, every nation had its presiding angel (cf. Daniel 10:13, 10:20–1). Michael, for instance, was held to be the guardian angel of Israel (Daniel 12:1). People, too, had their guardian angels. When Rhoda came with the news that Peter had escaped from prison, they would not believe her and said it was his angel (Acts 12:15). Jesus himself spoke of the angels who guard a little child (Matthew 18:10). If we take it in this sense, the difficulty is that then the guardian angels of the churches are being rebuked for the sins of the churches. In fact, Origen, the third-century biblical scholar, believed that this was the case. He said that the guardian angel of a church was like the tutor of a child. If a child went wrong, the tutor was blamed; and, if a church went wrong, God in his mercy blamed its angel. The difficulty is that, though the angel of the church is mentioned in the address of each letter, undoubtedly it is the members of the church who are being addressed.

(4) Both Greeks and Jews believed that every earthly thing had a heavenly counterpart; and it is suggested that the angel is the ideal of the church and that the churches are being addressed as their ideal selves to bring them back to the right way.

None of the explanations is fully satisfactory; but maybe the last is the best, for there is no doubt that in the letters the angel and the church are one and the same.

We now go on to study the letters to the seven churches. In each case, we shall give an outline of the history and the contemporary background of the city in which the church was; and, once we have studied the general background, we will go on to study each letter in detail.

THE LETTER TO EPHESUS

Revelation 2:1–7

To the angel of the church in Ephesus, write:

These things says he who holds the seven stars in his right hand and who walks in the midst of the seven golden lampstands.

I know your works – I mean your toil and your steadfast endurance, and I know you cannot bear evil men, and that you have put to the test those who call themselves apostles, and who are not, and have proved them liars. I know that you possess steadfast endurance. I know all that you have borne for my name's sake and I know that you have not been worn out by your efforts. All the same, I have this against you – that you have left your first love. Remember, then, whence you have fallen, and repent, and make your conduct such as it was at first. If you do not, I am coming to you, and I will remove your lampstand from its place, if you do not repent.

But you do possess this virtue – you hate the works of the Nicolaitans, which I too hate.

Let him who has an ear hear what the Spirit is saying to the churches. I will give to him who overcomes to eat of the tree of life, which is in the Paradise of God.

EPHESUS: FIRST AND GREATEST

Revelation 2:1–7 (*contd*)

WHEN we know something of the history of Ephesus and learn something about its conditions at this time, it is easy to see why it comes first in the list of the seven churches.

Pergamum was the official capital of the province of Asia, but Ephesus was by far its greatest city. It claimed as its proud title 'The first and the greatest metropolis of Asia'. A Roman writer called it *Lumen Asiae*, the Light of Asia. Let us look at the factors which gave it its pre-eminent greatness.

(1) In the time of John, Ephesus was the greatest harbour in Asia. All the roads of the Cayster Valley – the Cayster was the river on which it stood – converged upon it. But the roads came from further afield than that. It was at Ephesus that the road from the far-off Euphrates and Mesopotamia reached the Mediterranean, having come by way of Colosse and Laodicea. It was at Ephesus that the road from Galatia reached the sea, having come by way of Sardis. And from the south came the road from the rich Maeander Valley. Strabo, the ancient geographer, called Ephesus 'the Market of Asia' – and it may well be that, in Revelation 18:12–13, John was setting down a description of the varied riches of the market place at Ephesus.

Ephesus was the gateway of Asia. One of its distinctions, laid down by statute, was that when the Roman proconsul came to take up office as governor of Asia, he must disembark at Ephesus and enter his province there. For all the travellers and the trade, from the Cayster and the Maeander Valleys, from Galatia, from the Euphrates and from Mesopotamia, Ephesus was the highway to Rome. In later times, when the Christians were brought from Asia to be flung to the lions in the arena in Rome, Ignatius, the Bishop of Antioch, called Ephesus the Highway of the Martyrs.

Its position made Ephesus the wealthiest and the greatest city in all Asia – and, because it resembled so well John Bunyan's picture in *The Pilgrim's Progress*, it has been aptly called the Vanity Fair of the ancient world.

(2) Ephesus had certain important political distinctions. It was a *free city*. In the Roman Empire, certain cities were free cities; they had had that honour conferred upon them because of their services to the empire. A free city was within its own limits self-governing, and it was exempted from ever having Roman troops garrisoned there. It was an *assize town*. The Roman governors made periodic tours of their provinces; and, at certain specially chosen cities and towns, courts were held where the governor tried the most important cases. Further, each year, Ephesus held the most famous games in Asia, which attracted people from all over the province.

(3) Ephesus was the centre of the worship of Artemis or, as the Authorized Version calls her, Diana of the Ephesians. The Temple of Artemis was one of the seven wonders of the ancient world. It was 425 feet long by 220 feet wide; it had 120 columns, each sixty feet high and the gift of a king; and thirty-six of them were richly gilded and inlaid. Ancient temples consisted mostly of colonnades with only the centre portion roofed over. The centre portion of the Temple of Artemis was roofed over with cypress wood. The image of Artemis was one of the most sacred images in the ancient world. It was by no means beautiful but a squat, black, many-breasted figure, so ancient that no one knew where it had come from. We have only to read Acts 19 to see how precious Artemis and her temple were to Ephesus. Ephesus also had famous temples to the godhead of the Roman emperors Claudius and Nero, and in future years it was to

add temples to Hadrian and Severus. In Ephesus, the ancient religion was at its strongest.

(4) Ephesus was a notorious centre of superstition. It was famous for the *Ephesian Letters*, small objects and charms which were supposed to be infallible remedies for sickness, to bring children to those who were childless and to ensure success in any undertaking; and people came from all over the world to buy them.

(5) The population of Ephesus was very mixed. Its citizens were divided into six tribes. One consisted of those who were descendants of the original natives of the country; one consisted of those who were direct descendants of the original colonists from Athens; three consisted of other Greeks; and one, most probably, consisted of Jews. Besides being a centre of religion, the Temple of Artemis was also a centre of crime and immorality. The temple area was a recognized place offering asylum; criminals were safe if they could reach it. The temple possessed hundreds of priestesses who were sacred prostitutes. All this combined to make Ephesus a notoriously evil place. Heraclitus, one of the most famous of ancient philosophers, was known as 'the weeping philosopher'. His explanation of his tears was that no one could live in Ephesus without weeping at its immorality.

Such was Ephesus; a more unpromising soil for the sowing of the seed of Christianity can scarcely be imagined; and yet it was there that Christianity had some of its greatest triumphs. R. C. Trench, the nineteenth-century Archbishop of Dublin, writes: 'Nowhere did the word of God find a kindlier soil, strike root more deeply or bear fairer fruits of faith and love.'

Paul stayed longer in Ephesus than in any other city (Acts 20:31). It was with Ephesus that Timothy had a connection, so that he is called its first bishop (1 Timothy 1:3). It is in Ephesus that we find Aquila, Priscilla and Apollos (Acts 18:19, 18:24, 18:26). Surely Paul was closer to no one than to the Ephesian elders, as his farewell address so beautifully shows (Acts 20:17–38). Later on, John was the leading figure of Ephesus. Legend has it that he brought Mary the mother of Jesus to Ephesus and that she was buried there. When Ignatius of Antioch wrote to Ephesus, on his way to being martyred in Rome, he could write: 'You were ever of one mind with the apostles in the power of Jesus Christ.'

There can be few places which better prove the conquering power of the Christian faith.

We may note one more thing. We have spoken of Ephesus as the greatest harbour of Asia. Today there is little left of Ephesus but ruins, and it is now at least six miles from the sea. The coast is now a harbourless line of sandy beach, unapproachable by a ship. What was once the Gulf of Ephesus and the harbour is a marsh dense with reeds. It was always a battle to keep the harbour of Ephesus open because of the silt which the Cayster brings down. The battle was lost, and Ephesus vanished from the scene.

EPHESUS: CHRIST AND HIS CHURCH

Revelation 2:1–7 (contd)

JOHN begins the letter to Ephesus with two descriptions of the risen Christ.

(1) He holds the seven stars in his right hand. That is to say, Christ holds the churches in his hand. The word for *to hold* is *kratein*, and it is a strong word. It means that Christ has complete control over the church. If the church submits to that control, it will never go wrong; and more than that – our security lies in the fact that we are in the hand of Christ.

'They will never perish. No one will snatch them out of my hand' (John 10:28).

There is another point here which emerges only in the Greek. *Kratein* normally takes a genitive case after it (the case which in English we express by the word *of*) because, when we take hold of a thing, we seldom take hold of *the whole of it* but usually of *part of it*. When *kratein* takes an accusative after it, it means that the whole object is gripped within the hand. Here, *kratein* takes the accusative, and that means that Christ clasps the whole of the seven stars in his hand. That means he holds *the whole Church* in his hand.

We do well to remember that. It is not only *our* church which is in the hand of Christ; the *whole* Church is in his hand. When people put up barriers between church and church, they do what Christ never does.

(2) He walks in the midst of the seven golden lampstands. The lampstands are the churches. This expression tells us of Christ's tireless activity in the midst of his churches. He is not confined to any one of them; wherever men and women meet together to worship in his name, Christ is there.

John goes on to say certain things about the people of the church of Ephesus.

(1) The risen Christ praises their *toil*. The word is *kopos*, and it is a favourite New Testament word. Tryphena, Tryphosa and Persis all *work hard* in the Lord (Romans 16:12). The one thing that Paul claims is that he has *worked harder* than all (1 Corinthians 15:10). He is afraid that the Galatians may slip back and his *labour* should be in vain (Galatians 4:11). In each case – and there are many others – the word is either *kopos* or the verb *kopian*. The special characteristic of these words is that they describe the kind of toil which takes up all mental and physical effort that can be put into it. The Christian way is not for those who are afraid to break sweat. Christians are

to toil for Christ; and, even if physical toil is impossible, they can still toil in prayer.

(2) The risen Christ praises their *steadfast endurance*. Here is the word *hupomonē*, which we have come across again and again. It is not the grim patience which resignedly accepts things. It is the courageous gallantry which accepts suffering and hardship and turns them into grace and glory. It is often said that suffering colours life; but, when we meet life with the *hupomonē* which Christ can give, the colour of life is never grey or black; it is always tinged with glory.

EPHESUS: WHEN ORTHODOXY COSTS TOO MUCH

Revelation 2:1–7 (*contd*)

THE risen Christ goes on to praise the Christians of Ephesus because they have tested evildoers and proved them to be liars.

Many came into the little congregations of the early Church with evil intent. Jesus had warned of the false prophets who are wolves in sheep's clothing (Matthew 7:15). In his farewell speech to the elders of this very church at Ephesus, Paul had warned them that savage wolves would invade the flock (Acts 20:29). These evil people were of many kinds. There were messages from the Jews who sought to entangle Christians again in the law and who followed Paul everywhere, trying to undo his work. There were those who tried to turn liberty into licence. There were professional beggars who preyed on the charity of the Christian congregations. The church at Ephesus was even more open to these recurring menaces than any other church. It was on the highway to Rome and to the east, and what R. C. Trench called 'the whole rabble of evildoers' was liable to descend upon it.

More than once, the New Testament insists on the necessity of testing. John in his First Letter insists that the spirits who claim to come from God should be tested by their willingness to accept the incarnation in all its fullness (1 John 4:1–3). Paul insists that the Thessalonians should test all things and then hold on to that which is good (1 Thessalonians 5:21). He insists that, when the prophets preach, they are subject to the testing of the other prophets (1 Corinthians 14:29). Individuals cannot proclaim private views in the assembly of God's people; they must conform to the tradition of the Church. Jesus demanded the hardest test of all: 'You will know them by their fruits' (Matthew 7:15–20).

The church at Ephesus had faithfully applied its tests and had weeded out all evil and misguided individuals; but the trouble was that something had got lost in the process. 'I have this against you,' says the risen Christ, 'that you have left your first love.' That phrase may have two meanings.

(1) It can mean that the first enthusiasm has gone. Jeremiah speaks of the devotion of Israel to God in the early days. God says to the nation that he remembers 'the devotion of your youth, your love as a bride' (Jeremiah 2:2). There had been a honeymoon period, but the first flush of enthusiasm is past. It may be that the risen Christ is saying that all the enthusiasm has gone out of the religion of the church of Ephesus.

(2) It is much more likely that this means that the first fine rapture of love for the church community has gone. In the first days, the members of the church at Ephesus had really loved each other; disagreement had never reared its head; the heart was ready to be stirred and the hand was ready to help. But something had gone wrong. It may well be that heresy-hunting had killed love, and orthodoxy had been achieved at the price of fellowship. When that happens, orthodoxy has cost

too much. All the orthodoxy in the world will never take the place of love.

EPHESUS: THE STEPS ON THE
RETURN JOURNEY

Revelation 2:1-7 (*contd*)

In Ephesus, something had gone wrong. The earnest toil was there; the gallant endurance was there; the faultless orthodoxy was there; but the love had gone. So the risen Christ makes his appeal, and it is for the three steps of the return journey.

(1) First, he says *Remember*. He is not here speaking to someone who has never been inside the church; he is speaking to those who are inside but have somehow lost the way. Memory can often be the first step on the way back. In the distant country, the prodigal son suddenly remembered his home (Luke 15:17).

The American writer O. Henry has a short story. There was a young boy who had been brought up in a village; and in the village school he had sat beside a village girl, innocent and sweet. The boy found his way to the city, fell into bad company and became an expert pickpocket. He was on the street one day; he had just picked a pocket – a neat job, well done – and he was pleased with himself. Suddenly he saw the girl he used to sit beside at school. She was still the same – innocent and sweet. She did not see him; he took care of that. But suddenly he remembered what he had been, and realized what he was. He leaned his burning head against the cool iron of a lamp-post. 'God,' he said, 'how I hate myself.' Memory was offering him the way back.

William Cowper wrote:

> Where is the blessedness I knew
> When first I saw the Lord?
> Where is the soul-refreshing view
> Of Jesus and his word?

A verse like that may sound like nothing but tragedy and sorrow; but in fact it can be the first step of the way back, for the first step to putting things right is to realize that something has gone wrong.

(2) Second, he says *Repent*. When we discover that something has gone wrong, there is more than one possible reaction. We may feel that nothing can sustain its first brightness, and so accept what we consider inevitable. We may be filled with a feeling of resentment, and blame life instead of facing ourselves. We may decide that the old thrill is to be found along forbidden pathways and try to find spice for life in sin. But the risen Christ says: 'Repent!' Repentance is the admission that the fault is ours and the expression of sorrow that it is so. The prodigal's reaction is: 'I will get up and go to my father, and I will say to him "Father, I have sinned"' (Luke 15:18). It is Saul's cry of the heart when he realizes his folly: 'I have been a fool, and have made a great mistake' (1 Samuel 26:21). The hardest thing about repentance is the acceptance of personal responsibility for our failure, for once the responsibility is accepted the godly sorrow will surely follow.

(3) Third, he says *Do*. The sorrow of repentance is meant to drive people to two things. First, it is meant to drive them to fling themselves on the grace of God, saying only: 'God, be merciful to me a sinner.' Second, it is meant to drive them to action in order to bring forth fruits meant for repentance. No one has truly repented if he or she does the same things again. The American Baptist, Harry Emerson Fosdick, said that the great truth of Christianity is that 'no man need stay the way he

is'. The proof of repentance is a changed life, a life changed by our effort in co-operation with the grace of God.

EPHESUS: A RUINOUS HERESY

Revelation 2:1-7 (contd)

HERE, we meet a heresy which the risen Christ says that he hates and which he praises Ephesus for also hating. It may seem strange to attribute hatred to the risen Christ; but two things are to be remembered. First, if we love anyone with passionate intensity, we are bound to hate anything which threatens to ruin that person. Second, it is necessary to hate the sin but love the sinner.

The heretics we meet here are the Nicolaitans. They are only named, not defined. But we meet them again in Pergamum (verse 15). There, they are very closely connected with those 'who hold to the teaching of Balaam' – and that in turn is connected with eating things offered to idols and with immorality (verse 14). We meet precisely the same problem at Thyatira, where the wicked Jezebel is said to cause Christians to practise immorality and to eat things offered to idols.

First, we may note that this danger is coming not from outside the Church but from inside. The claim of these heretics was that they were not destroying Christianity but presenting an improved version.

Second, we may note that the Nicolaitans and those who hold to the teaching of Balaam were, in fact, one and the same. There is a play on words here. The name *Nicolaus*, the founder of the Nicolaitans, could be derived from two Greek words, *nikan*, *to conquer*, and *laos*, *the people*. *Balaam* can be derived from two Hebrew words, *bela*, *to conquer*, and *ha'am*, *the people*. The two names, then, are the same, and both can describe an evil teacher, who has won victory over the people and brought them under the influence of poisonous heresy.

In Numbers 25:1–5, we find a strange story in which the Israelites were seduced into illegal and sacrilegious unions with Moabite women and into the worship of Baal-peor, a seduction which, if it had not been sternly checked, might have ruined the religion of Israel and destroyed Israel as a nation. When we go on to Numbers 31:16, we find that this seduction is definitely attributed to the evil influence of Balaam. Balaam, then, in Israelite history stood for an evil person who seduced the people into sin.

Let us now see what the early church historians have to tell us about these Nicolaitans. The majority identify them with the followers of Nicolaus, the convert from Antioch, who was one of the seven, commonly called deacons (Acts 6:5). The idea is that Nicolaus went astray and became a heretic. Irenaeus, the second-century Bishop of Lyons, said of the Nicolaitans that 'they lived lives of unrestrained indulgence' (*Against Heresies*, 1:26:3). The third-century theologian Hippolytus said that he was one of the seven and that 'he departed from correct doctrine, and was in the habit of inculcating indifference of food and life' (*Refutation of Heresies*, 7:24). *The Apostolic Constitutions* (6:8) describe the Nicolaitans as 'shameless in uncleanness'. Another early Christian theologian, Clement of Alexandria, said that they 'abandon themselves to pleasure like goats ... leading a life of self-indulgence'. But he goes on to acquit Nicolaus of all blame and says that they distorted his saying 'that the flesh must be abused'. Nicolaus meant that the body must be kept under control; the heretics distorted it into meaning that the flesh can be used as shamelessly as a person wishes (*The Miscellanies*, 2:20). The Nicolaitans obviously taught loose living.

Let us see if we can identify their point of view and their teaching a little more precisely. The letter to Pergamum tells us that they seduced people into eating meat offered to idols and into immorality. When we turn to the decree of the Council of Jerusalem, we find that two of the conditions on which the Gentiles were to be admitted to the Church were that they were to abstain from things offered to idols and from immorality (Acts 15:28–9). These are the very conditions that the Nicolaitans broke.

They were almost certainly people who argued on these lines. (1) The law is ended; therefore, there are no laws, and we are entitled to do what we like. They confused Christian liberty with un-Christian licence. They were the very kind of people whom Paul urged not to use their liberty as an opportunity for self-indulgence (Galatians 5:13). (2) They probably argued that the body is evil anyway and that people could do what they liked with their bodies because it did not matter. (3) They probably argued that Christians were so completely defended by grace that they could do anything and come to no harm.

What lay behind this Nicolaitan distortion of the truth? The trouble was the necessary difference between Christians and the society in which they lived. The non-Christians had no hesitation in eating meat offered to idols, and it was set before them at every social occasion. Could a Christian attend such a feast? The non-Christians had no idea of chastity, and sexual relations outside marriage were accepted as completely normal and brought no shame. Must Christians be so very different? The Nicolaitans were suggesting that there was no reason why Christians should not come to terms with the world. The archaeologist and New Testament scholar Sir William Ramsay describes their teaching in this way: 'It was an attempt to effect a reasonable compromise with the established usages of the Graeco-Roman society and to retain as many as possible of those usages in the Christian system of life.' This teaching naturally affected the upper classes most because they had most to lose if they went all the way with the Christian demand. To John, the Nicolaitans were worse than those who were not Christians, for they were the enemy within the gates.

The Nicolaitans were not prepared to be different; they were the most dangerous of all heretics from a practical point of view, for, if their teaching had been successful, the world would have changed Christianity and not Christianity the world.

EPHESUS: THE GREAT REWARD

Revelation 2:1–7 (contd)

FINALLY, the risen Christ makes his great promise to those who overcome. In this picture, there are two very beautiful ideas.

(1) There is the idea of *the tree of life*. This is part of the story of the Garden of Eden; in the middle of the garden, there was the tree of life (Genesis 2:9); it was the tree of which Adam was forbidden to eat (Genesis 2:16–17). Eating its fruit would make human beings like God; and, because they ate from it, Adam and Eve were driven out of Eden (Genesis 3:22–4).

In later Jewish thought, the tree came to stand for that which truly gave life to individuals. Wisdom is a tree of life to those who lay hold of it (Proverbs 3:18); the fruit of the righteous is a tree of life (Proverbs 11:30); hope fulfilled is a tree of life (Proverbs 13:12); a tongue is a tree of life (Proverbs 15:4).

To this is to be added another picture. Adam was first forbidden to eat of the tree of life, and then he was barred from the garden so that the tree of life was lost forever. But it was a regular Jewish belief that, when the Messiah came and the new age dawned, the tree of life would be in the centre of all people, and those who had been faithful would eat of it. The wise man said: 'Those who do what is pleasing to him enjoy the fruit of the tree of immortality' (Sirach [Ecclesiasticus] 19:19). The Rabbis had a picture of the tree of life in paradise. Its boughs overshadowed the whole of paradise; it had 500,000 fragrant perfumes and its fruit as many pleasant tastes, every one of them different. The idea was that what Adam had lost the Messiah would restore. To eat of the tree of life means to have all the joys that the faithful conquerors will have when Christ reigns supreme.

(2) There is the idea of *paradise*, and the very sound of the word is lovely. It may be that we do not attach any very definite meaning to it; but, when we study the history of the word, and when we see how the great thinkers of the Church have used it, we come upon some of the most adventurous thinking the world has ever known.

(a) Originally, *paradise* was a Persian word. The Greek historian Xenophon wrote much about the Persians, and it was he who introduced the word into the Greek language. Originally, it meant a pleasure garden. When Xenophon is describing the state in which the Persian king lived, he says that he takes care that, wherever he resides, there are *paradises*, full of all the good and beautiful things the soil can produce (*Oeconomicus*, 4:13). *Paradise* is a lovely word to describe a thing of serene beauty.

(b) In the Septuagint, *paradise* has two uses. First, it is regularly used for the Garden of Eden (Genesis 2:8, 3:1). Second, it is regularly used of any stately garden. When Isaiah speaks of a *garden* that has no water, it is the word *paradise* that is used (Isaiah 1:30). It is the word used when Jeremiah says: 'Plant *gardens* and eat what they produce' (Jeremiah 29:5). It is the word used when the preacher says: 'I made myself gardens and parks, and planted in them all kinds of fruit trees' (Ecclesiastes 2:5).

(3) In early Christian thought, the word has a special meaning. In Jewish thought, after death, all souls went to Hades – a grey and shadowy place. Early Christian thought pictured an intermediate state between earth and heaven to which all people went and in which they remained until the final judgment. This place was described by Tertullian as a vast cavern beneath the earth. But there was a special part in which the patriarchs and the prophets lived – and that was paradise. The Jewish philosopher Philo describes it as a place 'vexed by neither rain, nor snow, nor waves, but which the gentle zephyr refreshes, breathing ever on it from the ocean'. As Tertullian saw it, only one kind of person went straight to this paradise, and that was the martyr. 'The sole key', he said, 'to unlock paradise is your own life's blood' (*Concerning the Soul*, 55).

Origen was one of the most adventurous thinkers the Church ever produced. He writes like this: 'I think that all the saints [*saints* means *Christians*] who depart from this life will remain in some place situated on the earth, which holy Scripture calls paradise, as in some place of instruction and, so to speak, classroom or school of souls ... If anyone indeed be pure in heart and holy in mind, and more practised in perception, he will by making more rapid progress, quickly ascend to a place in the air, and reach the kingdom of heaven, through these mansions [*stages*] which the Greeks called *spheres* and which holy Scripture calls *heavens* ... He will in the end follow him who has passed into the heavens, Jesus the Son of God, who said: "I will that where I am, these may be also." It is of this diversity of places he speaks, when he said: "In my Father's house are many mansions"' (*De Principiis*, 2:6).

The great early thinkers did not identify paradise with heaven; paradise was the intermediate stage, where the souls of the righteous were prepared for entering the presence of God. There is something very lovely here. Who has not felt that the leap from earth to heaven is too great for one step and that there is need for a gradual entering into the presence of God? Might it have been of this that Charles Wesley was thinking when he sang these lines in the final verse of his hymn 'Love Divine'?

> *Changed from glory into glory,*
>> Till in heaven we take our place,
>> Till we cast our crowns before thee,
>>> Lost in wonder, love, and praise.

(4) In the end, in Christian thought, paradise did not retain this idea of an intermediate state. It came to be equivalent to heaven. Our minds must turn to the words of Jesus to the dying and penitent thief: 'Today you will be with me in Paradise' (Luke 23:43). We are in the presence of mysteries about which it would be irreverent to dogmatize; but is there any better definition of paradise than to say that it is life forever in the presence of our Lord? As Ray Palmer's hymn, 'Jesus, these eyes have never seen', has it:

> When death these mortal eyes shall seal,
>> And still this throbbing heart,
>> The rending veil shall thee reveal
>>> All glorious as thou art –

and that is paradise.

THE LETTER TO SMYRNA

Revelation 2:8–11

> And to the angel of the church in Smyrna, write:
>> These things says the first and the last, who passed through death, and who came to life again.

I know the affliction and the poverty you endure – you are rich in spite of it – and I know the slanders which proceed from those who call themselves Jews and are not, but who are a synagogue of Satan. Have no fear of what you will have to go through. Behold! the devil is going to throw some of you into prison in order to test you, and you will have a time of affliction which will last for ten days. Show yourselves loyal to death, and I will give you the crown of life.

Let him who has an ear hear what the Spirit is saying to the churches. He who overcomes will not be hurt by the second death.

SMYRNA: THE CROWN OF ASIA

Revelation 2:8–11 (*contd*)

IF it was inevitable that Ephesus should come first in the list of the seven churches, it was only natural that Smyrna, its great rival, should come second. Of all the cities of Asia, Smyrna was the loveliest. It was known as the ornament of Asia, the crown of Asia and the flower of Asia. The Greek satirist Lucian said that it was 'the fairest of the cities of Ionia'. Aristides, the Greek Christian writer, who sang the praise of Smyrna with such splendour, spoke of 'the grace which extends over every part like a rainbow ... the brightness which pervades every part, and reaches up to the heavens, like the glitter of the bronze of armour in Homer'. It added to the charm of Smyrna that the west wind, the gentle zephyr, constantly blew through its streets. 'The wind', said Aristides, 'blows through every part of the city, and makes it as fresh as a grove of trees.' The constant west wind had only one disadvantage. The sewage of the city drained into the gulf on which the city stood, and the west wind tended to blow the smell back upon the city rather than out to sea.

Smyrna was magnificently situated. It stood at the end of the road which crossed Lydia and Phrygia and travelled out to the far east, and it commanded the trade of the rich Hermus valley. Inevitably, it was a great trading city. The city itself stood at the end of a long arm of the sea, which ended in a small land-locked harbour in the heart of the city. It was the safest of all harbours and the most convenient; and it had the added advantage that in time of war it could be easily closed by a chain across its mouth. It was fitting that on the coins of Smyrna there should be the image of a merchant ship ready for sea.

The setting of the city was equally beautiful. It began at the harbour; it crossed the narrow foothills; and then behind the city there rose the Pagos, a hill covered with temples and noble buildings which were spoken of as 'the Crown of Smyrna'. One traveller has described it as 'a queenly city crowned with towers'. Aristides likened Smyrna to a great statue with the feet in the sea, the middle parts in the plain and the foothills, and the head, crowned with great buildings, on the Pagos behind. He called it 'a flower of beauty such as earth and sun had never shown to mankind'.

Smyrna's history was very much connected to its beauty, for it was one of the very few planned cities in the world. It had been founded as a Greek colony as far back as 1000 BC. Round about 600 BC, disaster had befallen it, for then the Lydians had broken in from the east and destroyed it. For 400 years, Smyrna had been no city but merely a collection of little villages; then the Macedonian general Lysimachus had rebuilt it as a planned whole. It was built with great, straight, broad streets. Strabo, the Greek geographer, speaks of the handsomeness of the streets, the excellence of the paving and the great rectangular blocks in which it was built. Most famous of all the streets was the Street of Gold, which began with the Temple of Zeus and ended with the Temple of Cybele. It ran across the foothills of the Pagos at an angle; and, if the buildings which encircled the Pagos were the crown of Smyrna, the Street of Gold was the necklace round the hill.

Here we have an interesting and a significant thing which shows the care and knowledge with which John set down his letters from the risen Christ. The risen Christ is called 'the one who died and came to life'. That was an echo of the experience of Smyrna itself.

Smyrna had other claims to greatness. It was a free city, and it knew what loyalty was. Long before Rome was undisputed ruler of the world, Smyrna had thrown in its lot with Rome, never to waver in its faithfulness. The Roman statesman Cicero called Smyrna 'one of our most faithful and our most ancient allies'. In the campaign against Mithridates in the east, things had gone badly with Rome. And when the soldiers of Rome were suffering from hunger and cold, the people of Smyrna stripped off their own clothes to send to them.

Such was the reverence of Smyrna for Rome that, as far back as 195 BC, it was the first city in the world to build a temple to the goddess Roma. And in AD 26, when the cities of Asia Minor were competing for the privilege of erecting a temple to the godhead of Tiberius, Smyrna was picked out for that honour, overcoming even Ephesus.

Not only was Smyrna great in trade, beauty and political and religious status; it was also a city where culture flourished. Apollonius of Tyana had urged upon Smyrna the truth that only the people can make a city great. He said: 'Though Smyrna is the most beautiful of all cities under the sun, and makes the sea its own, and holds the fountains of the zephyr, yet it is a greater charm to wear a crown of men than a crown of porticoes and pictures and gold beyond the standard of mankind: for buildings are seen only in their own place, but men are seen everywhere and spoken about everywhere and make their city as vast as the range of countries which they can visit.' So Smyrna had a stadium in which famous games were held each year, a magnificent public library, an Odeion, which was the home of music, and a theatre which was one of the largest in Asia Minor. In particular, Smyrna was one of the cities which laid claim to being the birthplace of the Greek poet Homer; it had a memorial building called the Homereion, and put Homer's head on its coinage. This was a disputed claim. Thomas Heywood, the seventeenth-century poet, wrote the famous epigram:

> Seven cities warr'd for Homer, being dead,
> Who, living, had no roof to shroud his head.

In such a city, we would expect magnificent architecture; and in Smyrna there was a host of temples to Cybele, to Zeus, to Apollo, to Nemesis, to Aphrodite and to Asclepios.

Smyrna had rather more than its share of a characteristic which was common to all Greek cities. The German historian Theodor Mommsen said that Asia Minor was 'a paradise of municipal vanity', and Smyrna of all cities was noted for 'its municipal rivalry and its local pride'. Everyone in it wanted to exalt Smyrna and had a personal desire to climb to the top of the municipal tree. It is not without significance that in the address of the letter the risen Christ is called 'the first and the last'. In comparison with his glory, all earthly distinctions are worthless.

There remains one feature of Smyrna which stands out in the letter and which had serious consequences for the Christians there. The Jews were especially numerous and influential (verse 9). We find them, for instance, contributing 10,000 denarii to make the city beautiful. It is clear that in Smyrna they were particularly hostile to the Christian

Church, no doubt because it was from them and from those interested in Judaism that Christianity drew many of its converts. So, we may well end this study of Smyrna with the story of the most famous Christian martyrdom which happened there.

Polycarp, Bishop of Smyrna, was martyred on Saturday, 23rd February, AD 155. It was the time of the public games; the city was crowded, and the crowds were excited. Suddenly the shout went up: 'Away with the atheists; let Polycarp be searched for.' No doubt Polycarp could have escaped; but already he had had a dream in which he saw the pillow under his head burning with fire; and, when he woke, he told his disciples: 'I must be burnt alive.'

His whereabouts were betrayed by a slave who collapsed under torture. They came to arrest him. He ordered that they should be given a meal and provided with all they required, while he asked for himself the privilege of one last hour in prayer. Not even the police captain wanted to see Polycarp die. On the brief journey to the city, he pleaded with the old man: 'What harm is it to say: "Caesar is Lord" and to offer sacrifice and be saved?' But Polycarp was adamant that for him only Jesus Christ was Lord.

When he entered the arena, there came a voice from heaven saying: 'Be strong, Polycarp, and play the man.' The proconsul gave him the choice of cursing the name of Christ and making sacrifice to Caesar – or death. 'Eighty and six years have I served him,' said Polycarp, 'and he has done me no wrong. How can I blaspheme my King who saved me?' The proconsul threatened him with burning, and Polycarp replied: 'You threaten me with the fire that burns for a time, and is quickly quenched, for you do not know the fire which awaits the wicked in the judgment to come and in everlasting punishment. Why are you waiting? Come, do what you will.'

So the crowds came flocking from the workshops and from the baths with bundles of wood – and the Jews, even though they were breaking the Sabbath law by carrying such burdens, were ahead of everyone in bringing wood for the fire. They were going to bind him to the stake. 'Leave me as I am,' he said, 'for he who gives me power to endure the fire will grant me to remain in the flames unmoved even without the security you will give by the nails.' So they left him loosely bound in the flames, and Polycarp prayed his great prayer:

> O Lord God Almighty, Father of thy beloved and blessed Child, Jesus Christ, through whom we have received full knowledge of thee, God of angels and powers, and of all creation, and of the whole family of the righteous, who live before thee, I bless thee that thou hast granted unto me this day and hour, that I may share, among the number of the martyrs, in the cup of thy Christ, for the resurrection to eternal life, both of soul and body in the immortality of the Holy Spirit. And may I today be received among them before thee, as a rich and acceptable sacrifice, as thou, the God without falsehood and of truth, hast prepared beforehand and shown forth and fulfilled. For this reason I also praise thee for all things. I bless thee, I glorify thee through the eternal and heavenly High Priest, Jesus Christ, thy beloved Child, through whom be glory to thee with him and the Holy Spirit, both now and for the ages that are to come. Amen.

So much is plain fact; but then the story drifts into legend, for it goes on to tell that the flames made a kind of tent around Polycarp and left him untouched. At length, the executioner stabbed him to death to achieve what the flames could not do. 'And when he did this there came out a dove, and much blood, so that the fire was quenched, and all the crowd marvelled that there was such a difference between the unbelievers and the elect.'

What is certain is that Polycarp died a martyr for the faith.

It cannot have been easy to be a Christian at Smyrna – and yet the letter to Smyrna is one of the two in which there is undiluted praise.

SMYRNA: UNDER TRIAL

Revelation 2:8–11 (contd)

THE church of Smyrna was in trouble, and a further period of trial was imminent.

There are three things that the letter says about this trial.

(1) It is *thlipsis*, *affliction*. *Thlipsis* originally meant crushing beneath a weight. The pressure of events is on the church at Smyrna.

(2) It is *ptōcheia*, *poverty*. In the New Testament, poverty and Christianity are closely connected. 'Blessed are you who are poor,' said Jesus (Luke 6:20). Paul described the Christians at Corinth as being poor yet making many rich (2 Corinthians 6:10). James speaks of God choosing the poor in this world to be rich in faith (James 2:5).

In Greek, there are two words for *poverty*. *Penia* describes the state of those who are not wealthy and who, as the Greeks defined it, must satisfy their needs with their own hands. *Ptōcheia* describes complete destitution. It has been put this way: *penia* describes the state of someone who has nothing superfluous; *ptōcheia* describes the state of someone who has nothing at all.

The poverty of the Christians was due to two things. It was due to the fact that most of them belonged to the lower classes of society. The gulf between the top and the bottom of the social scale was very wide. We know, for instance, that in Rome the poorer classes literally starved because contrary winds delayed the corn ships from Alexandria, and the entitlement of corn could not be distributed to those in need.

There was another reason for the poverty of the Christians. Sometimes they suffered from the plundering of their possessions (Hebrews 10:34). There were times when a mob would suddenly attack the Christians and wreck their homes. Life was not easy for a Christian in Smyrna or anywhere else in the ancient world.

(3) There is *imprisonment*. John forecasts an imprisonment of *ten days*. That is not to be taken literally. *Ten days* was an expression for a short time which was soon to come to an end. So this prophecy is at the same time both a warning and a promise. Imprisonment is coming; but the time of trouble, although sharp, will be short. Two things are to be noted.

First, this is exactly the way in which persecution came. To be a Christian was against the law; but persecution was not continuous. The Christians might be left in peace for a long time; but at any moment a governor might develop a fit of administrative energy, or the mob might call out for a search to find the Christians – and then the storm broke. The terror of being a Christian was the uncertainty.

Second, imprisonment does not sound so bad to us. We might say: 'Imprisonment? Well, that is not as bad as death anyway.' But, in the ancient world, imprisonment was merely the prelude to death. People were only prisoners until they were led out to die.

SMYRNA: THE CAUSE OF THE TROUBLE

Revelation 2:8–11 (*contd*)

THE instigators of persecution were the Jews. Again and again in Acts, we see how the Jews stirred up the authorities against the Christian preachers. It happened at Antioch (Acts 13:50), at Iconium (Acts 14:2, 14:5), at Lystra (Acts 14:19) and at Thessalonica (Acts 17:5).

The story of what happened at Antioch shows us how the Jews often succeeded in moving the authorities to take action against the Christians (Acts 13:50). Round the Jewish synagogues gathered many 'god-fearers'. These were Gentiles who were not prepared to go the whole way and to become full converts but were attracted by the preaching of one God instead of many gods and were attracted especially by the purity of the Jewish ethic as compared with life in Roman society. In particular, women were attracted to Judaism for these reasons. Often these women were from the higher social levels, the wives of magistrates and governors, and it was through them that the Jews gained access to the authorities and persuaded them to persecute.

John calls the Jews the *synagogue of Satan*. He is taking a favourite expression of the Jews and reversing it. When the people of Israel met together, they loved to call themselves 'the assembly of the Lord' (Numbers 16:3, 20:4, 31:16). *Synagogue* is in Greek *sunagōgē*, which literally means a coming together, an assembly, a congregation. It is as if John said: 'You call yourselves the assembly of God when, in fact, you are the assembly of the devil.' Once, John Wesley, the founder of Methodism, said of certain people who were presenting a crude picture of God: 'Your God is my devil.' It is a terrible thing when religion becomes the means of evil things. It has happened. In the eighteenth century, in the days of the French Revolution, Madame Roland uttered her famous cry: 'Liberty, what crimes are committed in your name!' There have been tragic times when the same could be said about religion.

Six slanders were regularly levelled against the Christians.

(1) On the basis of the words of the sacrament – *this is my body, and this is my blood* – the story went about that the Christians were cannibals.

(2) Because the Christians called their common meal the *Agape*, the Love Feast, it was said that their gatherings were orgies of lust.

(3) Because Christianity did, in fact, often split families, when some members became Christians and some did not, the Christians were accused of 'tampering with family relationships'.

(4) Worshippers in the traditional ancient religions accused the Christians of atheism because they could not understand a worship which had no images of the gods such as they themselves had.

(5) The Christians were accused of being politically disloyal because they would not say: 'Caesar is Lord.'

(6) The Christians were accused of being fire-raisers because they foretold the end of the world in flames.

It was not difficult for maliciously minded people to circulate dangerous slanders about the Christian Church.

SMYRNA: CHRIST'S CLAIM AND CHRIST'S DEMAND

Revelation 2:8–11 (*contd*)

WE have seen that the church at Smyrna was battling with difficulties and threatened with worse to come. In view of that, the letter to Smyrna opens with two resounding titles of Christ which tell what he can offer to those who may be confronted with a situation such as the one that faced the Christians at Smyrna.

(1) Christ is the first and the last. In the Old Testament, that is a title belonging to God. 'I am the first,' Isaiah heard

God say, 'and I am the last' (Isaiah 44:6, 48:12). This title has two aspects. To Christians, it is a tremendous promise. Come what may, from the first day of life to the last, the risen Christ is with us. Of whom then shall we be afraid?

But, to the general population of Smyrna, it was a warning. They loved their city, calling it the first in Asia, and they were all striving as individuals to be one better than their neighbours. The risen Christ said: 'I am the first and the last.' Here is the death of human pride. Beside the glory of Christ, all human titles are of no importance and all human claims become ridiculous. When Julian, the Roman emperor, had failed in his attempt to banish Christianity and bring back the old gods, and when he was meeting his death in the attempt, he said: 'To shoulder Christ from out the topmost niche was not for me.' He recognized that he could not remove Christ from his true place above all others.

(2) Christ is the one who was dead and is alive again. The tenses of the verb are of prime importance. The Greek for *was* is *genomenos*, which means *became*. It describes what we might call a passing phase. Christ became dead; it was an episode through which he passed. In Greek, the verb which the Authorized Version translates as *is alive* is not a present tense but an aorist, which describes one action completed in the past. The right translation is *came to life again* (as in the Revised Standard Version), and the reference is to the event of the resurrection. The risen Christ is the one who experienced death and came to life again in the triumphant event of the resurrection, and who is alive for evermore. Here again, there are two aspects.

(a) The risen Christ is one who has *experienced* the worst that life could do to him. He had died in the agony of the cross. No matter what happened to the Christians of Smyrna, Jesus Christ had been through it. Jesus Christ can help because he knows what life is like at its worst and has experienced even the bitterness of death.

(b) The risen Christ has *conquered* the worst that life can do. He triumphed over pain and over death; and he offers us through himself the way to victorious living.

In this passage there is also a demand, and the demand is for *loyalty*, loyal even when death is the price to be paid. Loyalty was a quality of which the people of Smyrna knew something, for their city had flung in its lot with Rome when Rome's greatness was only a far-off possibility, and had never wavered from it in its allegiance, in fair weather and in foul. If all the other noble qualities of life were placed in the balance against it, loyalty would outweigh them all. It was the writer Robert Louis Stevenson's prayer that 'in all the chances of fortune, and down to the gates of death' we should be 'loyal and loving to one another'.

SMYRNA: THE PROMISED REWARD

Revelation 2:8–11 (*contd*)

JESUS CHRIST will be in no one's debt, and loyalty to him brings its own reward. In this passage, two rewards are mentioned.

(1) There is *the crown of life*. Again and again, the crown of the Christian is mentioned in the New Testament. Here and in James 1:12, it is the crown of *life*. Paul speaks of the crown of *righteousness* (2 Timothy 4:8) and of the crown of *boasting* (1 Thessalonians 2:19). Paul contrasts the immortal crown of the Christian with the fading crown of laurel which was the prize of the victor in the games (1 Corinthians 9:25), and Peter speaks of the unfading crown of glory (1 Peter 5:4).

Of in each of these phrases means *which consists of*. To win the crown of righteousness or glory or life is to be crowned with righteousness or glory or with life. But we must understand the idea behind this word *crown* (*stephanos*). In Greek, there are two words for *crown* – *diadēma*, which means the *royal crown*, and *stephanos*, which usually has something to do with *joy* and *victory*. It is not the royal crown which is being offered to Christians; it is the crown of joy and victory. *Stephanos* has many associations, and all of them contribute something to the riches of thought behind it.

(a) The first connection is with the victor's crown in the games. Smyrna had games which were famous all over Asia. As in the Olympic Games, the reward of the victorious athlete was the laurel crown. Christians can win the crown of victory in the contest of life.

(b) When someone had faithfully performed the work of a magistrate, at the end of the term of office that person was granted a crown. Those who throughout life faithfully serve Christ and their neighbours will receive their crown.

(c) The Roman world was in the habit of wearing crowns, or garlands of flowers, at banquets. In the end, if Christians are loyal, they will have the joy of sitting as guests at the banquet of God.

(d) The worshippers of the Greek and Roman gods were in the habit of wearing crowns when they approached the temples of their gods. In the end, if they have been faithful, Christians will have the joy of entering into the nearer presence of God.

(e) Some scholars have seen in this crown a reference to the halo or the nimbus which is round the head of divine beings in pictures. If that is so, it means that, if they are faithful, Christians will be crowned with the life which belongs to God himself. As John said: 'We will be like him, for we will see him as he is' (1 John 3:2).

In this life, it may be that their loyalty will bring Christians a crown of thorns; but in the life to come it will surely bring them the crown of glory.

(2) Cyprian, the third-century Bishop of Carthage, uses two great phrases to describe those who are faithful even to death. He describes them as 'illustrious with the heraldry of a good name', and he calls them 'the white-robed cohort of the soldiers of Christ'. To the faithful, another promise is made: they will not be hurt by the *second death*. The *second death* is a mysterious phrase which occurs nowhere in the New Testament outside Revelation (20:6, 20:14, 21:8). The Rabbis talked of 'the second death whereof the wicked die in the next world'. The phrase may have two origins.

(a) The Sadducees believed that after death there was absolutely nothing; the Epicureans, whose beliefs were based on the importance of pleasure, held the same doctrine. This belief finds its place even in the Old Testament – for that pessimistic book Ecclesiastes is the work of a Sadducee. 'A living dog is better than a dead lion. The living know that they will die, but the dead know nothing' (Ecclesiastes 9:4–5). For the Sadducees and the Epicureans, death was extinction. To orthodox Jews, this was too easy, for it meant that for the wise and for fools the end was the same (Ecclesiastes 2:15–16, 9:2). They, therefore, came to believe that there were, so to speak, two deaths – physical death, which everyone must undergo, and after that a death which was the judgment of God.

(b) This is very closely connected with the ideas which we touched on when studying the word *paradise* (2:7). We saw that many of the Jews and the early Christian thinkers believed that there was an intermediate state into which everyone passed until the time of judgment. If that were so, then indeed there would be two deaths – the physical death which no one can escape, and the spiritual death into which the wicked would enter after the final judgment.

Of such things it is not given to anyone to speak with confidence; but, when John spoke of the faithful being unharmed by the second death, he meant precisely the same as Paul when he said that nothing in life or in death, in the present time or in eternity, can separate those who love him from Jesus Christ. They are safe from all that life or death can do to them (Romans 8:38–9).

THE LETTER TO PERGAMUM

Revelation 2:12–17

And to the angel of the church in Pergamum, write:
These things says he who has the sharp two-edged sword.

I know where your home is. I know that it is where the throne of Satan is; and yet you hold fast to my name, and have not denied your loyalty to me, even in the days of Antipas, my faithful martyr, who was killed among you, where Satan has his home. But I have a few things against you. You have among you some people who hold the teaching of Balaam, who taught Balak to put a stumbling-block before the children of Israel, to eat meat offered to idols and to commit fornication. So you, too, have those who in the same way hold the teaching of the Nicolaitans. So, then, repent. If you do not, I am coming to you quickly, and I will go to war with them with the sword of my mouth.

Let him who has an ear hear what the Spirit is saying to the churches. To him who overcomes I will give a share of the hidden manna; and I will give him a white stone, and written on the stone a new name, which no one but him who receives it knows.

PERGAMUM: THE SEAT OF SATAN

Revelation 2:12–17 (*contd*)

THERE is a difference in the name of this city in the various translations of the New Testament. The Authorized Version calls it *Pergamos*, while the Revised Version, the Revised Standard Version and James Moffatt call it *Pergamum*. *Pergamos* is the feminine form of the name and *Pergamum* the neuter. In the ancient world, it was known by both forms; but, of the two, *Pergamum* was much the more commonly used, and the newer translations are right to prefer it.

Pergamum had a unique place in Asia. It was not on any of the great roads, as Ephesus and Smyrna were, but historically it was the greatest city in Asia. Strabo, the Greek geographer, called it an illustrious (*epiphanēs*) city, and Pliny, the Governor of Bithynia, called it 'by far the most famous city in Asia' (*longe clarissimum Asiae*). The reason was that, by the time John was writing, Pergamum had been a capital city for almost 400 years. Back in 282 BC, it was made the capital of the Seleucid kingdom, one of the sections into which the empire of Alexander the Great was broken up. It remained the capital until 133 BC. In that year, Attalus III died; and, before he died, he willed his dominions into the possession of Rome. Out of the dominions of Attalus, Rome formed the province of Asia, and Pergamum still remained its capital.

Its geographical position made Pergamum even more impressive. It was built on a tall conical hill which dominated the valley of the River Caicus, from the top of which the Mediterranean could be seen, fifteen miles away. The archaeologist Sir William Ramsay describes it thus: 'Beyond all other cities in Asia Minor, it gives the traveller the impression of a royal city, the home of authority; the rocky hill on which it stands is so huge, and dominates the broad plain of the Caicus so proudly and so boldly.' History and honour gathered around Pergamum. Let us then set down its outstanding characteristics.

(1) Pergamum could never achieve the commercial greatness of Ephesus or of Smyrna, but it was a centre of culture which surpassed both. It was famous for its library, which contained no fewer than 200,000 parchment rolls. It was second only to the unique library of Alexandria.

It is interesting to note that the word *parchment* is derived from *Pergamum*. In the ancient world, *parchment* was *hē pergamēnē charta, the Pergamene sheet*; and there is a story about this name. For many centuries, rolls were written on papyrus, a substance made of the pith of a very large bulrush which grows beside the Nile. The pith was extracted, cut into strips, pressed into sheets and smoothed. This process produced a substance not unlike brown paper, and this was universally used for writing. In the third century BC, a Pergamene king called Eumenēs was very anxious to make the library of the city supreme. In order to do so, he persuaded Aristophanes of Byzantium, the librarian at Alexandria, to agree to leave Alexandria and come to Pergamum. Ptolemy of Egypt, enraged at this seduction of his outstanding scholar, promptly imprisoned Aristophanes and by way of retaliation put an embargo on the export of papyrus to Pergamum. Faced with this situation, the scholars of Pergamum invented parchment or vellum, which is made of the skins of animals, smoothed and polished. In fact, parchment is a much superior substance on which to write; and, although it did not do so for many centuries, in the end it ousted papyrus altogether as a writing material.

(2) Pergamum was one of the great religious centres. In particular, it had two famous shrines. In the letter of

the risen Christ, Pergamum is said to be the place where 'Satan's seat' is. Obviously, this must refer to something which the Christian Church regarded as particularly evil. Some have found the reference explained in Pergamum's religious splendour.

(a) Pergamum regarded itself as the custodian of the Greek way of life and of Greek worship. About 240 BC, it had won a great victory against the savage invading Galatae, or Gauls. In memory of that victory, a great altar to Zeus was built in front of the Temple of Athene which stood 800 feet up on Pergamum's conical hill. Forty feet high, it stood on a projecting ledge of rock and looked exactly like a great throne on the hillside. All day, it smoked with the smoke of sacrifices offered to Zeus. Around its base was carved one of the greatest achievements in the world of sculpture, the frieze which showed the Battle of the Giants, in which the gods of Greece were victorious over the giants of the barbarians. It has been suggested that this great altar was Satan's seat. But it is unlikely that a Christian writer would call that altar Satan's seat, for even by this time the old Greek gods were anachronisms and it would have been a waste of breath for Christians to attack them.

(b) Pergamum was particularly connected with the worship of Asclepios, so much so that Asclepios was known as 'the Pergamene god'. When Galen was mentioning favourite oaths, he said that people commonly swore by Artemis of Ephesus, or Apollo of Delphi, or Asclepios of Pergamum. Asclepios was the god of healing, and his temples were the nearest thing to hospitals in the ancient world. From all over the world, people flocked to Pergamum for relief from their sicknesses. In his commentary, R. H. Charles has called Pergamum 'the Lourdes of the ancient world'. The task of healing was partly the work of the priests, partly the work of doctors – Galen, second only to Hippocrates in the medical history of the ancient world, was born in Pergamum – and partly the work of Asclepios himself. Was there anything in that worship to move the Christians to call the Temple of Asclepios Satan's seat? There may have been two things.

First, the most common and most famous title for Asclepios was *Asclepios Sōtēr*, Asclepios the Saviour. It might well be that the Christians felt a shudder of horror that the name *Saviour* should be given to anyone other than Jesus Christ, the Saviour of the world.

Second, the emblem of Asclepios was the serpent, which still appears on the cap badge of the Royal Army Medical Corps. Many of the coins of Pergamum have Asclepios' serpent as part of their design. It might well be that Jews or Christians would regard a religion which took the serpent as its emblem as a satanic cult. Again, this explanation seems unlikely. As has been pointed out, the Christians would regard the place where people went to be healed – and often were – with sympathy rather than with indignation. The worship of Asclepios surely would not give adequate grounds for calling Pergamum Satan's seat.

It seems, then, that we must look elsewhere for the explanation of this phrase.

(3) Pergamum was the administrative centre of Asia. That meant that it was the centre of Caesar-worship for the province. We have already described Caesar-worship and the dire dilemma in which it placed Christians (pp. 17–22).

It was organized with a provincial centre and an administration like that of a presbytery or diocese. The point here is that Pergamum was the centre of that worship for the province of Asia. Undoubtedly, that is why Pergamum was Satan's seat; it was the place where people were required on pain of death to take the name of *Lord* and give it to Caesar instead of to Christ; and to a Christian there could be nothing more satanic than that.

And here is the explanation of the beginning of the letter to Pergamum. The risen Christ is called *the one who has the sharp two-edged sword.* Roman governors were divided into two classes – those who had the *ius gladii*, the right of the sword, and those who did not. Those who had the right of the sword had the power of life and death; on their word a person could be executed on the spot. In terms of worldly power, the proconsul, who had his headquarters at Pergamum, had the *ius gladii*, the right of the sword, and at any moment he might use it against any Christian; but the letter tells Christians not to forget that the last word is still with the risen Christ, who has the sharp two-edged sword. The power of Rome might be satanically powerful; but the power of the risen Lord is even greater.

PERGAMUM: A VERY DIFFICULT ENGAGEMENT

Revelation 2:12–17 (*contd*)

To be a Christian in Pergamum was to face what Oliver Cromwell, the Lord Protector of England, would have called 'an engagement very difficult'.

We have already seen what a concentration of Greek religion there was in Pergamum. There was the worship of Athene and Zeus, with its magnificent altar dominating the city; there was the worship of Asclepios, bringing sick people from far and near; and above all there were the demands of Caesar-worship, hanging forever like a poised sword above the heads of the Christians.

So the risen Christ says to the Christians of Pergamum: 'I know where you stay.' The word for *to stay* is here *katoikein*; and it means to have one's permanent residence in a place. It is a very unusual word to use of Christians in the world. Usually the word used of them is *paroikein*, which means to be a non-resident or an exile. Peter writes his letter to the *exiles* throughout the provinces of Asia Minor. But here the matter is being looked at from another point of view. The Christians of Pergamum have their permanent residence, as far as this world is concerned, in Pergamum; and Pergamum is the place where Satan's rule is strongest.

Here is something very important. The principle of the Christian life is not escape but conquest. We may feel it would be very much easier to be a Christian in some other place and in some other circumstances; but the duty of Christians is to witness for Christ where life has set them. We once heard of a girl who was converted in an evangelistic campaign. She was a reporter on a secular newspaper, and her first step after her conversion was to get a new job on a small Christian newspaper where she was constantly in the company of committed Christians. It was strange that the first thing that her conversion did was to make her run away. The more difficult it is to be a Christian in any set of circumstances, the greater the obligation to remain within those circumstances. If in the early days Christians had run away every time they were confronted with a difficult engagement, there would have been no chance of a world for Christ.

The Christians at Pergamum proved that it was perfectly possible to be a Christian under such circumstances. Even when martyrdom was in the air, they did not flinch. Of Antipas we know nothing; there is a late legend in the writings of Tertullian that he met his death by being slowly roasted to death within a brass bull. But there is a point in the Greek – impossible to reproduce in English – which is extremely significant. The risen Christ calls Antipas *my faithful martus*. We have translated that as *martyr*; but *martus* is the normal Greek word for *witness*. In the early Church, to be a martyr and to be a witness were one and the same thing. *Witness* so often meant *martyrdom*. Here is a rebuke to us. So many are prepared to demonstrate their Christianity in Christian circles but are equally prepared to play it down in circles where Christianity is met with opposition.

We must note another thing. The risen Christ calls Antipas *my faithful martus* and so gives him nothing less than his own title. In Revelation 1:5 and 3:14, Christ himself is called *the faithful martus*; to those who are true to him he gives nothing less than his own name.

PERGAMUM: THE DOOM OF ERROR

Revelation 2:12–17 (*contd*)

In spite of the faithfulness of the church at Pergamum, there is error. There are those who hold the teaching of Balaam and the doctrine of the Nicolaitans. We have already discussed these people in connection with Ephesus, and we meet them again when we come to study the letter of Thyatira. They sought to persuade Christians that there was nothing wrong with a prudent conformity to the world's standards.

Those who are not prepared to be different need not start on the Christian way at all. The most common word for a Christian in the New Testament is *hagios*, whose basic meaning is *different* or *separate*. The Temple is *hagios* because it is *different* from other buildings; the Sabbath day is *hagios* because it is different from other days; God is supremely *hagios* because he is totally different from human beings; and the Christian is *hagios* because he or she is different from others.

We must be clear what this difference means, for there is a paradox in it. It is Paul's summons to the Corinthians that they should be different from the world. 'Come out from them' (2 Corinthians 6:17). This difference from the world does not involve separation from it or hatred for it. Paul says in writing to the very same church: 'I have become all things to all people, so that I might by any means save some' (1 Corinthians 9:22). It was Paul's claim that he could get on with and communicate with all kinds of people; but – and here is the point – his getting on with them was *that he might save some*. It was not a question of bringing Christianity down to their level; it was a question of bringing them up. The fault of the Nicolaitans was that they were following a policy of compromise solely to save themselves from trouble.

It is the word of the risen Christ that he will make war with them. We must note that he did not say: 'I will go to war with *you*'; he said: 'I will go to war with *them*.' His wrath was directed not against the whole Church but against those who were seducing it; for those who were led astray, he had nothing but pity.

It is the threat of the risen Christ that he will make war against them with *the sword of his mouth*. The Christ of the sword is a startling idea. Thinking of past conquerors and comparing them with Jesus Christ, the poet wrote:

> Then all these vanished from the scene,
>   Like flickering shadows on a glass;
> And conquering down the centuries came
>   The swordless Christ upon an ass.

What then is the sword of Christ? The writer to the Hebrews speaks of the word of God which is sharper than any two-edged sword (Hebrews 4:12). Paul speaks of 'the sword of the Spirit, which is the word of God' (Ephesians 6:17). The sword of Christ is the word of Christ.

In the word of Christ, there is *conviction of sin*; in it, we are confronted with the truth and thereby with our own failure to obey it. In the word of Christ, there is *invitation to God*; it convicts people of sin and then invites them back to the love of God. In the word of Christ, there is *assurance of salvation*; it convicts people of sin, it leads them to the cross and it assures them that there is no other name under heaven given among mortals by which we must be saved (Acts 4:12). The conquest of Christ is his power to win men and women to the love of God.

PERGAMUM: THE BREAD OF HEAVEN

Revelation 2:12–17 (*contd*)

IN this letter, the risen Christ promises two things to those who overcome; the first is a share of the *hidden manna* to eat. Here is a Jewish idea which has two aspects.

(1) When the children of Israel had no food in the desert, God gave them manna to eat (Exodus 16:11–15). When the need of the manna passed, the memory did not. A pot of the manna was put into the ark and set before God in the Holy of Holies in the tabernacle and in the Temple (Exodus 16:33–4; Hebrews 9:4). Early in the sixth century BC, the Temple which Solomon had built was destroyed; and the Rabbis had a legend that, when that happened, Jeremiah hid away the pot of manna in a cleft in Mount Sinai and that, when the Messiah came,

he would return and the pot of manna would be discovered again. To a Jew, 'to eat of the hidden manna' meant to enjoy the blessings of the messianic age. To a Christian, it meant to enter into the blessedness of the new world which would emerge when the kingdom came.

(2) There may be a wider and more general meaning. Of the manna, it is said: 'This is the bread that the Lord has given you to eat' (Exodus 16:15). The manna is called 'grain of heaven' (Psalm 78:24); and it is said to be the 'bread of angels' (Psalm 78:25). Here, the manna may mean *heavenly food*. In that case, John would be saying: 'In this world, you cannot share with the non-Christians in their feasts because you cannot sit down to meat which is part of a sacrifice that has been offered to an idol. You may think that you are being called upon to give up much, but the day will come when you will feast in heaven upon heavenly food.' If that is so, the risen Christ is saying that people must abstain from the seductions of earth if they want to enjoy the blessings of heaven.

(3) There is one possible further interpretation of this. Some have suggested that the hidden manna is the bread of God given to Christians at the sacrament of the Lord's Supper. John tells us that the Jews said to Jesus that their ancestors had eaten manna in the wilderness, so receiving bread to eat. He goes on to explain that Jesus said that only God could give the true bread from heaven and that he made the claim: 'I am the bread of life' (John 6:31–5). If the hidden manna and the bread of life are the same, the hidden manna not only is the bread of the sacrament but also stands for nothing less than Christ, the bread of life; and this is a promise that to those who are faithful he will give himself.

PERGAMUM: THE WHITE STONE AND
THE NEW NAME

Revelation 2:12–17 (*contd*)

THE final promise of Christ to the faithful in Pergamum is that he will give them the white stone with the new name on it. This is a passage of which there are almost endless interpretations. In the ancient world, a white stone might stand for many things.

(1) There was a Rabbinic legend that precious stones fell from heaven along with the manna. The white stone would then simply stand for the precious gifts of God to his people.

(2) In the ancient world, coloured stones were used as counters for doing calculations. This would mean that Christians are counted among the number of the faithful.

(3) In the ancient law courts, white and black stones were used for registering the verdicts of juries – black for guilty, white for not guilty. This would mean that Christians are acquitted in the sight of God because of the work of Jesus Christ.

(4) In the ancient world, objects called *tesserae* were much used. A *tessera* was a little tablet made of wood or metal or stone; it had writing on it; and, generally speaking, the possession of a *tessera* conferred some kind of privilege upon an individual. Three of these *tesserae* add something to the picture.

(a) In Rome, the great houses had their *clients*, dependants who each morning received from their patron food and money for the day. They were often given a *tessera* by which they identified themselves as having the right to the free gifts. This would mean that Christians have the right to the free gifts for life which Christ can give.

(b) To win a victory at the games was one of the greatest honours the ancient world could give. Outstanding victors were given, by the master of the games, a *tessera*, which in the days to come conferred upon them the right of free entry to all public entertainments. This would mean that Christians are the victorious athletes of Christ who may share in the glory of their Lord.

(c) In Rome, a great gladiator was a hero admired by everyone. Often, a gladiator had to fight on until he was killed in combat. But, if he had had a particularly illustrious career, when he grew old he was allowed to retire in honour. Such men were given a *tessera* with the letters SP on it. SP stands for the Latin word *spectatus*, which means *a man whose valour has been proved beyond a doubt*. This would mean that Christians are the gladiators of Christ and that, when they have proved their valour in the battle of life, they are allowed to enter into the rest which Christ gives with honour.

(5) In the ancient world, a particularly happy day was called *a white day*. The Greek historian Plutarch tells that, when Pericles was besieging Samos, he knew that the siege would be long. He did not want his army to grow weary, so he divided it into eight parts. Every day, the eight companies drew lots; one was a white bean; and the company which drew the white bean was exempt from duty for the day and could enjoy itself as it wished. So it was that a happy day came to be called a white day (*Life of Pericles*, 64). In one of his letters, Pliny tells a friend that that day he had had the joy of hearing in the law courts the cases made by two magnificent young advocates in whose hands the future of Roman oratory was safe; and, he says, that experience made that day one marked *candidissimo calculo*, with the whitest of stones (*Letters*, 6:11). It was said that the Thracians and the Scythians kept in their homes an urn into which for every happy day they threw a white stone and for every unhappy day a black stone. At the ends of their lives, the stones were counted; and, depending

on the greater number of white or black stones, a person was said to have had a wretched or a happy life. This would mean that, through Jesus Christ, Christians can have the joy that no one can take from them (John 16:22).

(6) Along this line, there is another and most likely interpretation. One of the most common of all customs in the ancient world was to carry a small lucky object, or charm. It might be made of a precious metal or a precious stone, but often it was nothing more than a pebble. On the pebble there was a sacred name; to know a god's name was to have a certain power over that god, to be able to summon him to one's aid in time of difficulty and to have control over the demons. Such an object was thought to be doubly effective if no one but the owner knew the name that was inscribed upon it. Most likely, what John is saying is: 'Your friends – and you did the same in the days before you became a Christian – carry charms with superstitious inscriptions on them and they think they will keep them safe. You need nothing like that; you are safe in life and in death because you know the name of the only true God.'

PERGAMUM: RENAMED BY GOD

Revelation 2:12–17 (contd)

IT is just possible that we ought to look for the meaning of the new name and the white stone in another direction altogether.

The words *white* and *new* are characteristic of Revelation. R. H. Charles has said that in Revelation 'white is the colour and livery of heaven'. The word used describes not a dull, flat whiteness but one which glistens like snow in the winter sun. So, in Revelation we find white garments (3:5), white robes

(7:9), white linen (19:8, 19:14) and the great white throne of God himself (20:11). White, then, is heaven's colour.

In Greek, there are two words for *new*. There is *neos*, which means new in point of time. A thing can be *neos* and yet exactly like any number of things. On the other hand, there is *kainos*, which is new not only in point of time but also in quality; nothing like it has ever been made before. So, in Revelation there is the new Jerusalem (3:12), the new song (5:9), the new heavens and the new earth (21:1); and God makes all things new (21:5). With this in mind, two lines of thought have been suggested.

It has been suggested that the white stone is the individual Christian; that the risen Christ is promising his faithful ones a new self, cleansed of all earthly stains and glistening with the purity of heaven.

As to the new name, one of the features of the Old Testament is the giving of a new name to mark a new status. So Abram becomes Abraham when the great promise is made that he will be the father of many nations and when he, as it were, acquires a new status in the plan of God for men and women (Genesis 17:5). So, after the wrestling at Peniel, Jacob becomes Israel, which means the prince of God, because he had prevailed with God (Genesis 32:28). Isaiah hears the promise of God to the nation of Israel: 'The nations shall see your vindication, and all the kings your glory; and you shall be called by a new name that the mouth of the Lord will give' (Isaiah 62:2).

This custom of giving a new name to mark a new status was familiar to Roman society as well. The name of the first of the Roman emperors was Octavius; but when he became emperor he was given the name Augustus to mark his new status.

A curious superstitious parallel to this comes from peasant life in Palestine. When someone was very ill and in danger of death, that person was often given the name of another person who had lived a long and saintly life, as if this turned the one who was sick into a new person over whom the illness might lose its power.

On this basis of interpretation, Christ promises a new status to those who are faithful to him.

This is attractive. It suggests that the white stone means that Jesus Christ gives to those who are true to him a new self and that the new name means the new status of glory into which those who have been true to Christ will enter when this life ends and when the next begins. It remains to be said that, attractive as that interpretation is, the view which traces back the white stone and the new name to the use of charms is more likely to be correct.

THE LETTER TO THYATIRA

Revelation 2:18–29

> And to the angel of the church in Thyatira, write:
> These things says the Son of God, who has eyes like a flame of fire and whose feet are like beaten brass.
> I know your works – I mean your love and your loyalty and your service and your steadfast endurance; and I know that your last works are more than your first.
> But I hold it against you that you make no effort to deal with the woman Jezebel, who calls herself a prophetess and whose misleading teaching causes my servants to commit fornication and to eat meat offered to idols. I have given her a time within which to repent and she refuses to repent from her fornication. Behold, I am going to cast her into a bed and I am going to cast her paramours into great affliction, unless they repent from

her deeds; and I will slay her children with death; and all the churches will know that I am he who searches the inmost desires and thoughts of a man's being; and I will give to each one of you what your works deserve.

To the rest of you in Thyatira, to all those who do not hold this teaching, to such as have not known the deep things of Satan, as they call them, I say this – I am not going to put any other burden on you. All I say is, hold on to what you have until I come.

I will give to him who overcomes, and who keeps my works to the end, authority over the Gentiles; and he will smite them with a rod of iron; like vessels of pottery they will be smashed; for this is the authority that I have received from my Father; and I will give him the morning star.

Let him who has an ear hear what the Spirit is saying to the churches.

THYATIRA: THE PERIL OF COMPROMISE

Revelation 2:18–29 (*contd*)

THE longest of the seven letters is written to the least important of the seven cities. Nonetheless, the problem which faced Thyatira and the danger which threatened it were those which were universally involved in the position of the Christians in Asia.

Thyatira lay in the long valley connecting the valleys of the Hermus and the Caicus rivers through which the railway runs today; and it was its geographical position which gave it its importance.

(1) Thyatira lay on the road which connected Pergamum with Sardis and went on to Philadelphia and to Laodicea, linking up with both Smyrna and Byzantium. That was the

road by which the imperial mail travelled; and it was crowded with the commerce of Asia and the east. Therefore, first and foremost, Thyatira was a great commercial town.

(2) Strategically, the importance of Thyatira was that it was the gateway to Pergamum, the capital of the province. The first we hear of Thyatira is that it is an armed garrison, protected by a company of Macedonian troops, placed there as an outpost to defend Pergamum. The difficulty was that Thyatira was not capable of any prolonged defence. It lay in an open valley. There was no height that could be fortified; and all that Thyatira could ever hope to do was to fight a delaying action until Pergamum could prepare to meet the invaders.

(3) Thyatira had no special religious significance. It was not a centre either of Caesar-worship or of Greek worship. Its local hero god was called Tyrimnus, and he appears on its coins on horseback armed with battle-axe and club. The only notable thing about Thyatira from the religious point of view was that it possessed a fortune-telling shrine, presided over by a female oracle called the Sambathē. Certainly, no threat of persecution hung over the Thyatiran church.

(4) What, then, was the problem in Thyatira? We know less about Thyatira than about any other of the seven cities and are, therefore, seriously handicapped in trying to reconstruct the situation. The one thing we do know is that it was a great commercial centre, especially of the dyeing industry and of the trade in woollen goods. It was from Thyatira that Lydia, the seller of purple, came (Acts 16:14). From inscriptions discovered, we learn that it had an extraordinary number of trade guilds. These were associations for mutual profit and pleasure of people employed in certain trades. There were guilds of workers in wool, leather, linen and bronze, makers of outer garments, dyers, potters, bakers and slave-dealers.

Here, we think, was the problem of the church in Thyatira. To refuse to join one of these guilds would mean to give up all prospect of commercial existence. Why should a Christian not join one of these guilds? They held common meals. These would very often be held in a temple; and, even if not, they would begin and end with a formal sacrifice to the gods, and the meat eaten would be meat which had already been offered to idols. Further, it often happened that these communal meals were occasions of drunken revelry and slack morality. Was it possible for a Christian to be part of such occasions?

Here was the problem at Thyatira: the threat came from inside the church. There was a strong movement, led by the woman referred to as Jezebel, which pleaded for compromise with the world's standards in the interests of business and commercial prosperity, maintaining, no doubt, that the Holy Spirit could preserve them from any harm. The answer of the risen Christ is uncompromising. Christians must have nothing to do with such things.

THYATIRA: THE STATE OF THE CHURCH IN THYATIRA

Revelation 2:18–29 (contd)

R. H. CHARLES points out that by far the longest of the seven letters is written to the most unimportant of the seven cities; but its problem was far from being unimportant.

Of all the seven letters, this is the most enigmatic. Our trouble is that we have so little definite information about Thyatira – and we are presented with a series of four questions. What was the situation of the church in Thyatira? Who was Jezebel? What did she teach? What do the promises made to the church at Thyatira mean?

First, the letter opens with a description of the risen Christ
which has a threat in it. His eyes are like a flame of fire and
his feet like polished bronze. The description is taken from
that of the angelic messenger in Daniel 10:6: 'His face [was]
like lightning, his eyes like flaming torches, his arms and
legs like the gleam of burnished bronze.' The flaming eyes
must stand for two things – blazing anger against sin and the
awful penetration of that gaze which strips the disguises away
and sees into the depths of a person's heart. The bronze feet
must stand for the immovable power of the risen Christ. A
message which begins like that will certainly be no soothing
tranquillizer.

The letter goes on to use terms of the highest praise. The
love and loyalty and service and endurance of the church at
Thyatira are matters for congratulation. We must note how
these great qualities go in pairs. Service is the outcome of
love, and patient endurance the product of loyalty.

Then comes the condemnation of the woman Jezebel
and all her ways and teaching; and one can hardly avoid the
conclusion that she had very considerable influence in the
church at Thyatira.

The only conclusion seems to be this. On the surface, the
church at Thyatira was strong and flourishing. A stranger who
went into it would be impressed with its abounding energy and
its generous liberality and its apparent steadfastness. For all
that, there was something essential missing.

Here is a warning. A church which is crowded with people
and which is a hive of energy is not necessarily a real church.
It is possible for a church to be crowded because its people
come to be entertained instead of instructed, and to be soothed
instead of confronted with the fact of sin and the offer of
salvation; it may be a highly successful Christian club rather
than a real Christian congregation.

THYATIRA: THE SOURCE OF THE ERROR

Revelation 2:18–29 (*contd*)

SECOND, the source of the trouble in Thyatira centred round a woman whom the letter calls Jezebel. A variety of answers have been given to the question of her identity.

(1) We begin with an answer which is very interesting, although it is doubtful if it is possible. The Authorized Version calls her *that woman Jezebel*. James Moffatt's translation has 'that Jezebel of a woman'. The Greek is *tēn gunaika Iezebel*. After *gunaika*, a few manuscripts have the word *sou*, which means *your*. The noun *gunē* – the nominative of the word of which *gunaika* is the accusative form – means not only *woman* but also *wife*; and, if with these manuscripts we read *tēn gunaika sou Iezebel*, the phrase will mean *your wife Jezebel*.

Earlier on, we saw that the *angel* of the church may be the *bishop* of the church. If, then, the letter is addressed to the bishop of the church and there is a reference to *your wife Jezebel*, it means that the cause of all the trouble is the bishop's wife! But this interpretation must be rejected because the evidence for inserting *sou* is not good enough.

(2) One of the few claims to distinction which Thyatira possessed was an oracle called the *Sambathē*, a female fortune-teller. The Greeks made great use of oracles. The oracle at Delphi was world-famous, and the expression *a Delphic utterance* has become proverbial. It may be that this oracle was Jewish, for the Jews in the ancient world went in largely for this business of fortune-telling. There are those who see in the Sambathē the evil influence which was threatening the church at Thyatira; but this, too, must be rejected, for it is quite clear that Jezebel was a member of the church, and her influence was being exerted from within.

(3) Some, on no grounds whatever, have identified Jezebel with Lydia, the seller of purple from Thyatira, whom Paul met and converted at Philippi. It is suggested that she came back to Thyatira and became an evil influence in the church because of her wealth and her business interests. That theory is merely a slander on Lydia.

(4) The only reasonable conclusion is that we have no idea who Jezebel was, although we can with certainty trace the kind of person that she was.

That she claimed to be a prophetess is not so very surprising. It is true that Paul would have nothing to do with women speaking in the church (1 Corinthians 14:34). But it is also true that in both the Old and the New Testaments there are prophetesses. In the Old Testament, there are Miriam (Exodus 15:20), Deborah (Judges 4:4) and Huldah (2 Kings 22:14); and in the New Testament there are Anna (Luke 2:36) and the four virgin daughters of Philip (Acts 21:9).

This woman is called *Jezebel* and, therefore, her character must be discovered in the original Jezebel, than whom few women have acquired a worse reputation for wickedness. She was the daughter of Ethbaal, king of Sidon, and the wife of Ahab (1 Kings 16:31). When she came from Sidon, she brought her own gods and caused Ahab and his people to worship Baal. It was not that she would have wanted to banish the worship of Yahweh, if the prophets of Yahweh would have accepted Baal *in addition to* Yahweh. She slew the prophets of the Lord and at her own table supported 450 prophets of Baal (1 Kings 18:13, 18:19). She was Ahab's evil genius; in particular, she was responsible for the murder of Naboth in order that Ahab might gain possession of the ground where his vineyard stood (1 Kings 21). And she left behind her a name for 'whoredoms and sorceries' (2 Kings 9:22).

All this must mean that Jezebel of Thyatira was an evil influence on the life and worship of the Christian Church. It must be clearly understood that she had no wish to destroy the Church; but she wanted to bring into it new ways which were, in fact, destructive of the faith.

THYATIRA: THE TEACHING OF JEZEBEL (1)

Revelation 2:18–29 (*contd*)

THIRD, this Jezebel is accused of teaching two things – eating meat offered to idols and committing fornication.

(1) One of the great problems of the Christian Church was that of meat offered to idols, and it was one which Christians encountered every day. When a sacrifice was made in a Greek temple, very little of the meat was burned on the altar. Sometimes, all that was actually burned was a few hairs cut from the forehead of the animal. The priests received a share of the meat of the animal as their 'perk'; and the worshipper received the rest and did one of two things. A feast might be held within the temple precincts for the worshipper's friends. A common form of invitation to a festal meal ran: 'I invite you to dine with me at the table of our Lord Serapis.' Or the meat might be taken home and a feast held in the worshipper's house. Here was the Christian problem. Could a Christian, in a temple or anywhere else, eat meat which had been consecrated to idols? Paul discusses this very problem in 1 Corinthians 8–10.

The problem was complicated by the fact that even the meat in butchers' shops might well have been offered to idols previously. The priests in the temples could not possibly consume all the meat which came their way, and therefore they sold much of their share to the butchers' shops. Such meat was the best meat. What was a Christian going to do about that?

The Church had no doubt as to where a Christian's duty lay. Abstention from things offered to idols was one of the conditions on which the Gentiles received the right of entry into the Christian Church (Acts 15:29).

The prohibition of meat offered to idols had one far-reaching consequence. It came near to cutting off Christians from all social fellowship with non-Christians; there were few social occasions, and almost no banquets, which they could share with non-Christians.

This had another consequence which, as we have already said, we think was behind the situation in Thyatira. It meant that Christians could not join any trade guild, for all the guilds had a common meal as a central part of their practice, which might well be held in a Greek or Roman temple and would largely consist of meat offered to idols. Christians' abstention from guild membership was equivalent to commercial suicide.

Here is where Jezebel came in. She urged upon the Christians that there was no need to cut themselves off from society or abstain from the guilds. When she did so, she was not proceeding on grounds of principle but was simply trying to protect her business interests. Jezebel is to be counted among those to whom the claims of commercial success speak more loudly than the claims of Christ.

THYATIRA: THE TEACHING OF JEZEBEL (2)

Revelation 2:18–29 (contd)

(2) THE other part of Jezebel's teaching is not so clear. She is said to teach the people to commit fornication (verse 20); she is urged to repent from her fornication (verse 21); and those who

commit adultery with her and her children are threatened along with her (verses 22–3). Is this reference to be taken literally or in the metaphorical sense which is so common in Scripture to sexual immorality or to spiritual infidelity?

(a) There is no doubt that, in Scripture, infidelity to God is expressed in terms of fornication and adultery. Israel is the Bride of God (Isaiah 54:5; Jeremiah 3:20); and in the New Testament the Church is the Bride of Christ (2 Corinthians 11:1–2; Ephesians 5:24–8). Again and again in the Old Testament, the Israelites are, therefore, said to 'prostitute themselves to the foreign gods' (Deuteronomy 31:16; cf. Exodus 34:15–16; Hosea 9:1). In the New Testament, the age which is unfaithful to Jesus Christ is an 'evil and adulterous generation' (Matthew 12:39, 16:4; Mark 8:38). Is the *fornication* for which Jezebel's teaching argued a spiritual infidelity to Jesus Christ? If that is the meaning, her *paramours*, those who committed adultery with her (verse 22), will be those who are flirting with this kind of teaching, and her *children* (verse 23) will be those who have accepted it.

It may well be that the teaching of Jezebel was that the Christians did not need to be so exclusive in their worship of Jesus Christ and, above all, that there was no need for them to refuse to say: 'Caesar is Lord', and to burn their pinch of incense. If the Christian Church as a whole had accepted that form of teaching, the inevitable consequence would have been that Christianity would have become nothing other than yet one more of those religions of which the Roman Empire was so full. The claim of Christianity is not that Jesus Christ is one of the Saviours, nor even the chief of Saviours, but that he is the only Saviour.

(b) One thing in the letter militates against that view. We read that the followers of Jezebel claimed to know *the depths of Satan* (verse 24). Some scholars think that this is the risen

Christ's contemptuous description of the false teaching. The real Christian knows what Paul called the deep things of God (1 Corinthians 2:10); what Jezebel and her company know are the deep things of Satan. But that will not do, for the letter unmistakably speaks of 'the deep things of Satan, as *they* call them'. This is quite certainly a reference to a kind of belief that was not uncommon among the heretics. Some of them held that it was a plain duty to experience every kind of sin. The real achievement was to allow the body to wallow in sin and to keep the soul unaffected. Those who knew the deep things of Satan were those who had deliberately plumbed evil to its depths. Jezebel may well have been teaching that it was a duty to sin.

It seems to us that in this case all the threads tie up and there is no necessity to make a choice between views. There is every likelihood that Jezebel was teaching that Christians ought to accommodate themselves to the world; in other words, she was urging on the Church a spiritual infidelity which was bound to result in physical adultery. It is in the mercy of God that the teaching of Jezebel and those like her did not become the view of the Church. If that had happened, the Church would have become a kind of pleasant paganism. On this, Paul said: 'Do not be conformed to this world, but be transformed by the renewing of your minds' (Romans 12:2). And Jesus said the last word on the matter: 'No one can serve two masters ... You cannot serve God and wealth' (Matthew 6:24). The old choice is still the new choice: 'Choose this day whom you will serve' (Joshua 24:15; cf. Deuteronomy 30:19).

THYATIRA: PROMISES AND THREATS

Revelation 2:18–29 (*contd*)

FOURTH, the letter to Thyatira finishes with a series of great threats and great promises. Jezebel has been given all the leeway that the divine mercy can give her. If she does not repent, she will be cast into a bed of sickness, and her followers and those who commit adultery with her will share her fate. This will prove to everyone that indeed the risen Christ 'searches minds and hearts'. The phrase echoes the words of Jeremiah 11:20. In Jeremiah, the prerogative of searching the deepest thoughts of men and women belongs to God; but in Revelation, as so often, the prerogatives of God have become the prerogatives of the risen Christ. When the risen Christ says that he will search minds and hearts, it means that every emotion and every thought will be open to his gaze.

There is a real point here. When we began to study the letter to Thyatira, we saw that anyone coming into that church for the first time would have believed it to be surging with life and fruitful in every good work. No doubt those who prospered in business because of their compromise with the world were lavish in their generosity. No doubt those who attended the trade guilds gave freely to charitable funds. They *looked* like real Christians. No doubt Jezebel seemed to many to be a fine character. She must have had a command of language and a fine presence to be regarded as a prophetess. The point here is that the risen Christ can see beyond the outward disguise; he will know whether or not her repentance is real.

To those who are faithful, the promise is made; and it is twofold.

(1) The first part comes from Psalm 2:8–9: 'Ask of me, and I will make the nations your heritage, and the ends of the earth your possession. You shall break them with a rod of iron, and dash them in pieces like a potter's vessel.' In Jewish belief, that was a messianic psalm, thinking of a conquering Messiah who would smash the Gentiles and extend the rule of Israel to the ends of the earth. But it has also been one of the great missionary inspirations of the Christian Church. Many

missionaries have claimed that promise: 'Ask of me, and I will make the nations your heritage.'

(2) The second part is the promise of the morning star. Four main interpretations have been given.

(a) It is taken as a promise of the first resurrection. As the morning star rises after the night, so Christians will rise after the night of death.

(b) It is taken as the conquest of Lucifer. Lucifer is the devil, the angel who was so proud that he rebelled against God and was cast out of heaven (Isaiah 14:12). *Lucifer* means *light-bringer*, and it is the name of the morning star. If that is so, this is a promise of complete power over Satan and over sin.

(3) This has been referred to in Daniel 12:3. There, the promise is: 'Those who are wise shall shine like the brightness of the sky, and those who lead many to righteousness, like the stars for ever and ever.' If that is so, the morning star is the glory which will come to those who are righteous and have helped others to walk in the paths of righteousness.

(4) All these are very lovely and may all be involved in this promise; but we are quite certain that the correct interpretation is this. Revelation itself calls Jesus 'the bright morning star' (Revelation 22:16). The promise of the morning star is the promise of Christ himself. If Christians are true, when life comes to an end they will possess Christ, never to lose him.

THE LETTER TO SARDIS

Revelation 3:1–6

And to the angel of the church in Sardis, write:
　　These things says he who has the seven Spirits of God
　　and the seven stars.

I know your works; I know that you have a reputation for life, but that you are dead. Show yourself watchful, and strengthen what remains and what is going to die. I have not found your works completed before my God. Remember, then, how you received and heard the gospel, and keep it, and repent. If, then, you are not on the watch, I will come as a thief, and you will not know at what hour I will come to you.

But you have a few people in Sardis who have not defiled their garments and they will walk with me in white raiment, because they are worthy. He who overcomes will be thus clothed in white raiment and I will not wipe his name out of the Book of Life, but I will acknowledge his name before my Father and before his angels.

Let him who has an ear hear what the Spirit is saying to the churches.

SARDIS: PAST SPLENDOUR AND PRESENT DECAY

Revelation 3:1-6 (contd)

THE archaeologist Sir William Ramsay said of Sardis that nowhere was there a greater example of the melancholy contrast between past splendour and present decay. Sardis was a city of degeneration.

Seven centuries before this letter was written, Sardis had been one of the greatest cities in the world. There, the king of Lydia ruled over his empire in splendour. At that time, Sardis was a city of the east and was hostile to the Greek world. Aeschylus, the Greek poet, wrote of it: 'They that dwelt by Tmolus pledged themselves to cast the yoke on Hellas.'

Sardis stood in the middle of the plain of the valley of the River Hermus. To the north of that plain rose the long ridge of Mount Tmolus; from that ridge, a series of hills went out like spurs, each forming a narrow plateau. On one of these spurs, 1,500 feet up, stood the original Sardis. Clearly, such a position made it almost impregnable. The sides of the ridge were smoothly precipitous; and only where the spur met the ridge of Mount Tmolus was there any possible approach into Sardis, and even that was difficult and steep. It has been said that Sardis stood like some gigantic watch-tower guarding the Hermus valley. The time came when the narrow space on the top of the plateau was too small for the expanding city; and Sardis grew around the foot of the spur on which the citadel stood. The name Sardis (*Sardeis* in Greek) is really a plural noun, for there were two towns, one on the plateau and one in the valley beneath.

The wealth of Sardis was legendary. Through the lower town flowed the River Pactolus, which was said in past days to have had gold-bearing waters from which much of the wealth of Sardis came. The greatest of the Sardian kings was Croesus, whose name is still commemorated in the saying 'as rich as Croesus'. It was with him that Sardis reached the highest point in its history, and it was with him that it plunged to disaster.

It was not that Croesus was not warned about where Sardis was heading. Solon, the Athenian law-giver and the wisest of the Greeks, came on a visit and was shown the magnificence and the luxury. He saw the blind confidence of Croesus and his people that nothing could end this splendour, but he also saw that the seeds of softness and of degeneration were being sown. And it was then that he uttered his famous saying to Croesus: 'Call no man happy until he is dead.' Solon knew only too well the chances and changes of life which Croesus had forgotten.

Croesus embarked upon a war with Cyrus of Persia which was the end of the greatness of Sardis. Again Croesus was warned, but he failed to see the warning. To get at the armies of Cyrus, he had to cross the River Halys. He took counsel of the famous oracle at Delphi and was told: 'If you cross the River Halys, you will destroy a great empire.' Croesus took it as a promise that he would annihilate the Persians; it never crossed his mind that it was a prophecy that the campaign on which he had embarked would be the end of his own power.

He crossed the Halys, engaged in battle and was routed. He was not in the least worried, for he thought that all he had to do was to retire to the impregnable citadel of Sardis, recuperate and fight again. Cyrus initiated the siege of Sardis, waited for fourteen days, then offered a special reward to anyone who would find an entry into the city.

The rock on which Sardis was built crumbled easily. It was more like close-packed dried mud than rock. The nature of the rock meant that it developed cracks. A certain Mardian soldier called Hyeroeades had seen a Sardian soldier accidentally drop his helmet over the battlements and then make his way down the precipice to retrieve it. Hyeroeades knew that there must be a crack in the rock there by means of which an agile man could climb up. That night, he led a party of Persian troops up by the fault in the rock. When they reached the top, they found the battlements completely unguarded.

The Sardians had thought themselves too safe to need a guard; and so Sardis fell. A city with a history like that knew what the risen Christ was talking about when he said: 'Watch!'

There were a few futile attempts at rebellion; but Cyrus followed a deliberate policy. He forbade any Sardian to possess a weapon of war. He ordered them to wear tunics and buskins, that is, actors' boots, instead of sandals. He ordered them to teach their sons lyre-playing, the song and the dance, and retail trading. Sardis had been flabby already; but the last vestige of spirit was banished from its people, and it became a city of degeneration.

It vanished from history under Persian rule for two centuries. In due course, it surrendered to Alexander the Great, and through him it became a city of Greek culture. Then history repeated itself. After the death of Alexander, there were many claimants for the power. Antiochus, who became the ruler of the area in which Sardis stood, was at war with a rival called Achaeus who sought refuge in Sardis. For a year, Antiochus besieged him; then a soldier called Lagoras repeated the exploit of Hyeroeades. At night, with a band of brave men, he climbed the steep cliffs. The Sardians had forgotten their lesson. There was no guard, and once again Sardis fell because it had not kept watch.

Later, the Romans came. Sardis was still a wealthy city. It was a centre of the wool trade; and it was claimed that the art of dyeing wool was actually discovered there. It became a Roman assize town. In AD 17, it was destroyed by an earthquake which devastated the area. Tiberius, the Roman emperor, in his kindness cancelled all tribute money due for five years and gave a donation of 10,000,000 sesterces towards rebuilding – and Sardis recovered itself by the easy way.

When John wrote his letter to Sardis, it was wealthy but degenerate. Even the once great citadel was now only an ancient monument on the hilltop. There was no life or spirit there. The once great Sardians were soft, and twice they had lost their city because they were too lazy to keep watch. In that atmosphere so lacking in energy or concern, the Christian church too had lost its vitality and was a corpse instead of a living church.

SARDIS: DEATH IN LIFE

Revelation 3:1–6 (*contd*)

In the introduction to this letter, the risen Christ is described in two phrases.

(1) He is the one who has the seven Spirits of God. We have already come upon this strange phrase in Revelation 1:4. There are two aspects to its meaning. (a) It denotes the Holy Spirit with his sevenfold gifts, an idea founded on the description of the Spirit in Isaiah 11:2. (b) It denotes the Spirit in his sevenfold operation. There are seven churches, yet in each of them the Spirit operates with all his presence and power. The *seven spirits* signify the completeness of the gifts of the Spirit and the universality of his presence.

(2) He is the one who has the seven stars. The stars stand for the churches and their angels. The Church is the possession of Jesus Christ. People often act as if the Church belonged to them; but it belongs to Jesus Christ, and all its members are his servants. In any decision regarding the Church, the decisive factor must be not what any individual wants the Church to do but what Jesus Christ desires to be done.

The terrible accusation against the church at Sardis is that, although it has a reputation for life, it is in fact spiritually dead. The New Testament frequently likens sin to death. In the Pastoral Epistles, we read: '[She] who lives for pleasure is dead even while she lives' (1 Timothy 5:6). The prodigal son is the one who was dead and is alive again (Luke 15:24). The Roman Christians are described as having been brought from death to life (Romans 6:13). Paul says that his converts in their pre-Christian days were dead through trespasses and sins (Ephesians 2:1, 2:5).

(1) Sin is the *death of the will*. If someone accepts the invitations of sin for long enough, the time comes when that person cannot accept anything else. Habits grow until they can no longer be broken. People come, as the Roman philosopher Seneca had it, to hate their sins and to love them at the same time. There can be few of us who have not experienced the power of some bad habit into which we have fallen.

(2) Sin is the *death of the feelings*. The process of becoming the slave of sin does not happen overnight. The first time we sin, we do so with considerable qualms. But the day comes, if we go on taking what is forbidden, when we do something without a second thought that once we would have been horrified to do. Sin, as Robert Burns had it in his 'Epistle to a Young Friend', 'petrifies the feeling'.

(3) Sin is the *death of all loveliness*. The terrible thing about sin is that it can take the loveliest things and turn them into ugliness. Through sin, the yearning for the highest can become the craving for power; the wish to serve can become the intoxication of ambition; the desire of love can become the passion of lust. Sin is the killer of life's loveliness.

It is only by the grace of God that we can escape the death of sin.

SARDIS: A LIFELESS CHURCH

Revelation 3:1–6 (*contd*)

THE lifelessness of the church at Sardis had a strange effect.

(1) The church at Sardis was untroubled by any heresy. Heresy is always the product of the inquiring mind; it is, in fact, the sign of a church that is alive. There is nothing worse than a situation in which people are orthodox because they are too lazy to think for themselves. They are actually better with

a heresy which they hold intensely than with an orthodoxy about which in their heart of hearts they do not care.

(2) The church at Sardis was untroubled by any attack from the outside, whether by those who worshipped the gods of Greece and Rome, or by the Jews. The truth was that it was so lifeless that it was not worth attacking. The Pastoral Epistles describe those who had drifted away from the true faith by saying that they had a form of godliness but denied its power (2 Timothy 3:5). James Moffatt translates it: 'Though they keep up a form of religion, they will have nothing to do with it as a force.' J. B. Phillips translates it: 'They will maintain a façade of "religion", but their conduct will deny its validity.'

A church that is truly alive will always be under attack. 'Woe to you', said Jesus, 'when all speak well of you' (Luke 6:26). A church with a positive message is bound to be one to which there will be opposition.

A church which is so lethargic as to fail to produce a heresy is mentally dead; and a church which is so negative as to fail to produce opposition is dead in its witness to Christ.

SARDIS: WATCH!

Revelation 3:1-6 (contd)

IF anything is to be rescued from the impending ruin of the church in Sardis, the Christians there must wake from their deadly lethargy and watch. No commandment appears more frequently in the New Testament than the commandment to watch.

(1) Watchfulness should be the constant attitude of the Christian life. 'It is now the moment', says Paul, 'for you to wake from sleep' (Romans 13:11). 'Keep alert, stand firm in your faith', he urges (1 Corinthians 16:13). It has been

said that 'eternal vigilance is the price of liberty' and eternal watchfulness is the price of salvation.

(2) Christians must be on the watch against the cunning ways of the devil (1 Peter 5:8). The history of Sardis had its vivid examples of what happens to the garrison whose watch is slack. Christians are under continual attack by the powers which seek to seduce them from their loyalty to Christ. Often these attacks are subtle. They must, therefore, always be on the look-out.

(3) Christians must be on the watch against temptation. 'Stay awake and pray', said Jesus, 'that you may not come into the time of trial' (Matthew 26:41). Temptation waits for our unguarded moments and then attacks. In the Christian life, there must be unceasing vigilance against it.

(4) Repeatedly, the New Testament urges Christians to be alert and on the watch for the coming of their Lord. 'Keep awake therefore,' said Jesus, 'for you do not know on what day your Lord is coming.' 'And what I say to you I say to all: Keep awake' (Matthew 24:42; Mark 13:37). 'Let us not fall asleep as others do,' writes Paul to the Thessalonians, 'but let us keep awake and be sober' (1 Thessalonians 5:6). None of us knows the day and the hour when for us eternity will invade time. 'The last day is a secret,' says St Augustine, 'that every day may be watched.' We should live every day as if it were our last.

(5) Christians must be on the watch against false teaching. In Paul's last address to the elders of Ephesus, he warns them that savage wolves will invade the flock from outside, and from inside will arise those who will distort the truth. 'Therefore,' he says, 'be alert' (Acts 20:29–31).

(6) Nor must Christians forget that, even as they must watch for Jesus Christ, Jesus Christ is watching them. 'I have not found your works perfect', says the risen Christ, 'in the

sight of my God.' Here, two great truths meet us. (a) Christ is looking for something from us. We so often regard him as the one to whom we look for things; for his strength, his help, his support, his comfort. But we must never forget that he is looking for our love, our loyalty and our service. (b) The things we must do lie in our own hands. The old saying is true: 'Fate is what we must do; destiny is what we are meant to do.' Christians do not believe in an inescapable fate; but they do believe in a destiny which they can accept or refuse.

From every one of us, Jesus Christ is looking for something; and for every one of us there is something to do.

SARDIS: THE IMPERATIVES OF THE RISEN LORD

Revelation 3:1–6 (contd)

IN verse 3, we have a series of imperatives.

(1) The risen Christ says: '*Remember* how you received and heard the gospel.' It is the present imperative and means: 'Keep on remembering; never allow yourself to forget.' The risen Christ is telling the lethargic Sardians to remember the thrill with which they first heard the good news. It is a fact of life that certain things sharpen memory which has grown dull. When, for instance, we return to a graveside, the sorrow from which the years have taken the edge grows piercingly poignant again. Time and time again, Christians must stand before the cross and remember again what God has done for them.

(2) The risen Christ says: '*Repent!*' This is an aorist imperative and describes one definite action. In the Christian life, there must be a decisive moment when a person decides to finish with the old ways and to begin on the new.

(3) The risen Christ says: '*Keep* the commands of the gospel.' Here again, we have a present imperative indicating continuous action. It means: 'Never stop keeping the commands of the gospel.' Here is a warning against what we might call 'spasmodic Christianity'. Too many of us are Christian one moment and un-Christian the next.

(4) There is the command *to watch*. There is an old Latin saying that 'the gods walk on feet that are wrapped in wool'. Their approach is silent and unobserved, until people find themselves, without warning, facing eternity. But that cannot happen if every day men and women live in the presence of Christ; those who walk hand in hand with Christ cannot be taken unawares by his coming.

SARDIS: THE FAITHFUL FEW

Revelation 3:1–6 (*contd*)

IN verse 4, there shines through the darkness a ray of hope. Even in Sardis, there are the faithful few. When Abraham is pleading with God for Sodom, he appeals to God: 'Far be it from you ... to slay the righteous with the wicked' (Genesis 18: 25). In the old story of the kings, Abijah, alone of all the sons of Jeroboam, was spared because in him was found something pleasing to the Lord God of Israel (1 Kings 14:13). God never abandons his search for the faithful few, and they are never lost to his sight in the mass of the wicked.

It is said of the faithful that they 'have not soiled their garments'. James spoke with respect and admiration for those who kept themselves 'unstained by the world' (James 1:27). There are two possible pictures here.

(1) In the Gentile world, no worshipper was allowed to approach a temple of the gods with soiled clothes. For those concerned, this was an outwardly physical matter; but this may

describe those who have kept their souls clean so that they can enter into the presence of God and not be ashamed.

(2) H. B. Swete thinks that the white garments stand for the vow made at baptism, and that the phrase described those who had not broken their baptismal vows. At this stage in the Church's history, baptism was adult baptism, and at baptism individuals took a personal pledge to Jesus Christ. This is all the more likely because it was common for those who had been baptized, after they had emerged from the water, to be clothed in clean white robes, symbolic of the cleansing of their lives. Those who are faithful to their pledge will, beyond a doubt, some day hear God say: 'Well done!'

To those who have been true, the promise is that they will walk with God. Again, there is a double background.

(a) There may be another background from the world outside Christianity. At the Persian court, the king's most trusted favourites were given the privilege of walking in the royal gardens with the king and were called 'the Companions of the Garden'. Those who have been true to God will some day walk with him in paradise.

(b) There may be a reference to the old story of Enoch. 'Enoch walked with God; then he was no more, because God took him' (Genesis 5:24). Enoch walked with God on earth and continued to walk with him in the heavenly places. Those whose walk with God is close on earth will enter into a nearer companionship with him when the end of life comes.

SARDIS: THE THREEFOLD PROMISE

Revelation 3:1–6 (*contd*)

To those who have been faithful comes the threefold promise.

(1) They will be clothed with white garments. It is said of the righteous that they 'will shine like the sun in the kingdom of their Father' (Matthew 13:43); and it is said of God that he covers himself with light as with a garment (Psalm 104:2). What do the white robes signify?

(a) In the ancient world, white robes stood for *festivity*. 'Let your garments always be white,' said the preacher, 'do not let oil be lacking on your head' (Ecclesiastes 9:8). The white robes may stand for the fact that the faithful will be guests at the banquet of God.

(b) In the ancient world, white robes stood for *victory*. On the day when a Roman triumph was celebrated, all the citizens dressed themselves in white; the city itself was called *urbs candida*, the city in white. The white robes may stand for the reward of those who have won the victory.

(c) In any land and time, white is the colour of *purity*, and the white robes may stand for the purity whose reward is to see God. 'Blessed are the pure in heart, for they will see God' (Matthew 5:8).

(d) It has been suggested that the white robes stand for *the resurrection bodies* which the faithful will some day wear. Those who are faithful will share in that whiteness of light which is the garment of God himself.

We need not make a choice between these various meanings; we may well believe that they are all included in the greatness of the promise.

(2) Their names will not be wiped out of the book of life. The book of life is an idea which occurs often in the Bible. Moses is willing to be wiped out of the book which God has written, if by his sacrifice he can save his people from the consequence of their sin (Exodus 32:32–3). It is the hope of the psalmist that the wicked will be blotted out of the book of the living (Psalm 69:28). In the time of judgment, those who

are written in the book will be delivered (Daniel 12:1). The names of Paul's fellow labourers for God are written in the book of life (Philippians 4:3). The one who is not written in the book of life is cast into the lake of fire (Revelation 20:15); only they who are written in the Lamb's book of life shall enter into blessedness (Revelation 21:27).

In the ancient world, a king kept a register of his citizens. When someone committed a crime against the state, or when someone died, the name of that person was erased from that register. To have one's name written in the book of life is to be numbered among the faithful citizens of the kingdom of God.

(3) Jesus Christ will confess their names before his Father and the angels. It was Jesus' promise that whoever acknowledged him before others would be acknowledged by Jesus before his Father; and if anyone denied him before others, he would deny that person before his Father (Matthew 10:32–3; Luke 12:8–9). Jesus Christ is always true to those who are true to him.

THE LETTER TO PHILADELPHIA

Revelation 3:7–13

And to the angel of the church in Philadelphia, write:
These things says he who is holy, he who is true, he who has the key of David, he who opens and no man will shut, and shuts and no man opens. I know your works. Behold, I have set before you a door which stands open and which no man shuts, because you have a little strength, and because you have kept my word, and have not denied my name. Behold, I will give you those who belong to the synagogue of Satan, who call themselves Jews and who are not, but who lie. Behold,

I will make them come and kneel before your feet, and they will know that I have loved you. Because you have kept my command to endure, I, too, will keep you safe from the hour of testing, which is to come upon the whole inhabited world, to test those who dwell upon the earth. I am coming quickly. Hold on to what you have, that no one may take your crown.

I will make him who overcomes a pillar in the temple of my God and he will go out no more; and I will write upon him the name of my God, and the name of the city of my God, of the new Jerusalem, which is coming down from heaven from my God, and my new name.

Let him who has an ear hear what the Spirit is saying to the churches.

PHILADELPHIA: CITY OF PRAISE

Revelation 3:7–13 (*contd*)

PHILADELPHIA was the youngest of all the seven cities. It was founded by colonists from Pergamum under the reign of Attalus II, who ruled in Pergamum from 159 to 138 BC. *Philadelphos* is the Greek for *one who loves his brother*. Such was the love of Attalus for his brother Eumenes that he was called Philadelphos, and it was after him that Philadelphia was named.

It was founded for a special purpose. It was situated where the borders of Mysia, Lydia and Phrygia met. But it was not as a garrison town that Philadelphia was founded, for there was little danger there. It was founded with the deliberate intention that it might be a means of spreading Greek culture and language to Lydia and Phrygia; and so well did it do its work that by AD 19 the Lydians had forgotten their own language and were all but Greeks. The archaeologist Sir William Ramsay says of Philadelphia that it was 'the centre for the diffusion of Greek language and Greek letters in a peaceful land and by peaceful means'. That is what the risen Christ means when he speaks of the open door that is set before Philadelphia. Three centuries before, Philadelphia had been given an open door to spread Greek ideas in the lands beyond; and now there has come to it another great missionary opportunity, to carry to those who had yet to hear it the message of the love of Jesus Christ.

Philadelphia had one particular characteristic which has left its mark upon this letter. It was on the edge of a great plain called the *Katakekaumenē*, which means the Burned Land. The *Katakekaumenē* was a great volcanic plain bearing the marks of the lava and the ashes of volcanoes then extinct. Such land is fertile; and Philadelphia was the centre of a great grape-growing area and a famous producer of wines. But that situation had its perils, and these perils had left their mark more deeply on Philadelphia than on any other city. In AD 17, there was a great earthquake which destroyed Sardis and ten other cities. In Philadelphia, the tremors went on for years; Strabo describes it as a 'city full of earthquakes'.

It often happens that, when a great earthquake comes, people meet it with courage and self-possession, but the constantly recurring minor shocks drive them to sheer panic. That is what happened in Philadelphia. Strabo describes the scene. Shocks were an everyday occurrence. Gaping cracks appeared in the walls of the houses. First one part of the city was in ruins, then another. Most of the population lived outside the city in huts and were afraid even to go on to the city streets in case they should be killed by falling masonry. Those who still dared to live in the city were considered mad; they spent their time shoring up the shaking buildings and every now and then fleeing to the open spaces for safety. These terrible days in Philadelphia were never wholly forgotten, and people in the city were always waiting subconsciously for the ominous tremors of the ground, ready to flee for their lives to the open spaces. People in Philadelphia knew very well what security lay in a promise that 'they would go out no more'.

But there is more of Philadelphia's history than that in this letter. When this earthquake devastated it, Tiberius was as generous to Philadelphia as he had been to Sardis. In gratitude, it changed its name to Neocaesarea – the New City of Caesar. In the time of Vespasian, Philadelphia was to change its name, again out of gratitude, to Flavia, for Flavius was the emperor's family name. It is true that neither of these new names lasted and 'Philadelphia' was restored. But the people of Philadelphia knew what it was to receive 'a new name'.

Of all the cities, Philadelphia receives the greatest praise – and it was to show that it deserved it.

Later on, it became a very great city. When the Turks and Muslims flooded across Asia Minor, and every other town had fallen, Philadelphia stood firm. For centuries, it was a free Greek Christian city amid people from a very different culture. It was the last bastion of Asian Christianity. It was not until midway through the fourteenth century that it fell; and to this day there is a Christian bishop and 1,000 Christians in it. With the exception of Smyrna, the other churches are in ruins; but Philadelphia still holds aloft the banner of the Christian faith.

PHILADELPHIA: TITLES AND CLAIMS

Revelation 3:7-13 (contd)

In the introduction to this letter, the risen Christ is called by three great titles, each of which implies a tremendous claim.

(1) He is the one who is holy. Holy is the description of God himself. 'Holy, holy, holy is the Lord of hosts' was the song of the seraphs which Isaiah heard (Isaiah 6:3). 'To whom then will you compare me, or who is my equal? says the Holy One' (Isaiah 40:25). 'I am the Lord, your Holy One, the Creator of Israel, your King' (Isaiah 43:15). All through the Old Testament, God is the Holy One; and now that title is given to the risen Christ. We must remember that *holy* (*hagios*) means *different*, *separate from*. God is holy because he is different from us; he has that quality of being which belongs to him alone. To say that Jesus Christ is holy is to say that he shares the being of God.

(2) He is the one who is true. In Greek, there are two words for *true*. There is *alēthēs*, which means *true* in the sense that a true statement is different from a false statement. There is *alēthinos*, which means *real* as opposed to that which is unreal. It is the second of these words which is used here. In Jesus, there is reality. When we are confronted with him, we are confronted with no shadowy outline of the truth but with the truth itself.

(3) He is the one who has the key of David, who opens and no one will shut, who shuts and no one opens. We may first note that the key is *the symbol of authority*. Here is the picture of Jesus Christ as the one who has the final authority which no one can question.

Behind this, there is an Old Testament picture. Hezekiah had a faithful steward called Eliakim, who had authority over all his house and who alone could admit to the presence of the king. Isaiah heard God say of this faithful Eliakim: 'I will place on his shoulder the key of the house of David; he shall open, and no one shall shut; he shall shut, and no one shall open' (Isaiah 22:22). It is this picture which is in John's mind. Jesus alone has authority to admit to the new Jerusalem, the new city of David. As the *Te Deum* has it: 'Thou didst open the kingdom of Heaven to all believers.' He is the new and living way into the presence of God.

PHILADELPHIA: THE OPEN DOOR

Revelation 3:7–13 (*contd*)

IN verses 8–9, there is a problem of punctuation. In the early Greek manuscripts, there was no punctuation at all. The problem is that the words 'because you have a little strength, and because you have kept my word, and have not denied my name' can go equally well with what precedes them or with what follows. They may express either the reason why the door stands open before the Christians of Philadelphia or the reason why they will be given to those who belong to the synagogue of Satan. We have taken them with the words which precede them.

It is the great promise of the risen Christ that he has set before the Christians of Philadelphia an open door which no one can ever shut. What is the meaning of this open door?

(1) It may be the door of missionary opportunity. Writing to the Corinthians of the work which lies ahead of him, Paul says: 'For a wide door for effective work has opened to me' (1 Corinthians 16:9). When he came to Troas, a door was opened to him by the Lord (2 Corinthians 2:12). He asks the Colossians to pray that a door for the word may be opened for him (Colossians 4:3). When he came back to Antioch, he told how God had opened the door of faith to the Gentiles (Acts 14:27).

This meaning is particularly appropriate for Philadelphia. We have seen how it was a border town, standing where the boundaries of Lydia, Mysia and Phrygia met, and founded to be a means of passing on the Greek language and culture to the barbarous peoples beyond. It was on the road of the imperial postal service, which left the coast at Troas, came to Philadelphia via Pergamum, Thyatira and Sardis, and joined the great road out to Phrygia. The armies of Caesar travelled that road; the caravans of the merchants travelled it; and now it was beckoning the missionaries of Christ.

Two things emerge here. (a) There is a door of missionary opportunity before every one of us, and we need not go overseas to find it. Within the home, within the circle in which we move, within the parish in which we reside, there are those to be won for Christ. To use that door of opportunity is both our privilege and our responsibility. (b) In the way of Christ, the reward of work well done is more work to do. Philadelphia had proved faithful, and the reward for its fidelity was still more work to do for Christ.

(2) It has been suggested that the door which is set before the Philadelphians is none other than Jesus himself. 'I am the gate,' said Jesus (John 10:7, 10:9).

(3) It has been suggested that the door is the door to the Messianic community. With Jesus Christ, the new kingdom of David was inaugurated; and, just as in the ancient kingdom Eliakim had the keys to admit people to the royal presence, so Jesus is the door to admit people to the kingdom of God.

(4) Apart from all these things, the door of prayer is always open to anyone. That is a door which no one can ever shut, and it is one which Jesus opened when he assured us of the seeking love of God the Father.

PHILADELPHIA: INHERITORS OF THE PROMISE

Revelation 3:7-13 (contd)

IN verse 9, the promise of the risen Christ is that some day the Jews who slander the Christians will kneel before them. This is an echo of an expectation of the Jews which finds frequent expression in the Old Testament.

The expectation was that, in the new age, all nations would do humble homage to the Jews. This promise recurs again and again in Isaiah. 'The descendants of those who oppressed you shall come bending low to you, and all who despised you shall bow down at your feet' (Isaiah 60:14). 'The wealth of Egypt and the merchandise of Ethiopia and the Sabeans, tall of stature, shall come over to you and be yours, they shall follow you; they shall come over in chains and bow down to you' (Isaiah 45:14). 'Kings shall be your foster-fathers, and their queens your nursing-mothers. With their faces to the ground they shall bow down to you, and lick the dust of your feet' (Isaiah 49:23). Zechariah has a vision of the day when all people of all nations and languages shall turn to Jerusalem: they 'shall take hold of a Jew, grasping his garment and saying, "Let us go with you, for we have heard that God is with you"' (Zechariah 8:23).

It was the Christian belief that the Jewish nation had lost its place in God's plan and that that place had passed to the Church. A Jew in God's sense of the term was not one who could claim racial descent from Abraham but one of any nation who had made the same venture of faith as Abraham had made (Romans 9:6–9). The Church was the Israel of God (Galatians 6:16). It was, therefore, now true that all the promises which had been made to Israel had been inherited by the Church. It was to the Church that one day all people would humbly make their submission. This promise is a reversal of all that the Jews had expected; they had expected that all nations would kneel before them; but the day was to come when, with all nations, they too would kneel before Christ.

That is what the Philadelphian church would see, at least in its beginnings, if its members were faithful. Up until now, they had been faithful. In the sentence 'You have kept my word, and have not denied my name', both the verbs are in the aorist tense, which describes one definite act in past time; and the implication is that there had been some time of trial out of which the Philadelphian church had emerged triumphantly true. They may have only a little strength; their resources may be small; but, if they are faithful, they will see the dawn of the triumph of Christ. The one thing which must keep Christians faithful is the vision of a world for Christ, for the coming of such a world depends on the faithfulness of every individual Christian.

PHILADELPHIA: THOSE WHO KEEP ARE KEPT

Revelation 3:7–13 (*contd*)

IT is the promise of the risen Christ that those who keep will be kept. 'You have kept my commandment,' he says, 'therefore, I will keep you.' Loyalty has its sure reward. In verse 10, in the Greek, the phrase *my command to endure* is highly concentrated. Literally, it is *the word of my endurance*. The real meaning is that the promise is to those who have practised the same kind of endurance as Jesus displayed in his earthly life.

When we are called upon to show endurance, the endurance of Jesus Christ supplies us with three things. First, it supplies us with an example. Second, it supplies us with an inspiration. We must live looking always to him who, for the joy that was set before him, endured the cross, despising the shame (Hebrews 12:1–2). Third, the endurance of Jesus Christ is the guarantee of his sympathy with us when we are called upon to endure. 'Because he himself was tested by what he suffered, he is able to help those who are being tested' (Hebrews 2:18).

In verse 10, we are back again amid beliefs which are characteristically Jewish. As we have so often seen, the Jews divided time into two ages – the present age, which is wholly bad, and the age to come, which is wholly good, with in between the terrible time of destruction when judgment will fall upon the world. It is to that terrible time that John refers. Even when time comes to an end, and the world as we know it ceases to exist, those who are faithful to Christ will still be safe in his keeping.

PHILADELPHIA: PROMISE AND WARNING

Revelation 3:7–13 (*contd*)

In verse 11, there is promise and warning combined.

The risen Christ tells them that he is coming quickly. It has been said that in the New Testament the coming of Christ is continually used for two purposes.

(1) It is used as *a warning to the heedless*. Jesus himself tells of the wicked servant, who took advantage of his master's absence to beat his slaves and to get drunk, and to whom the master made a sudden return that brought judgment (Matthew 24:48–51). Paul warns the Thessalonians of the terrible fate which awaits the disobedient and the unbelieving when the Lord Jesus shall be revealed from heaven and shall take swift and final vengeance on his enemies (2 Thessalonians 1:7–9). Peter warns his people that they will give account for their deeds to the one who comes to judge the living and the dead (1 Peter 4:5).

(2) It is used as a *comfort to the oppressed*. James urges patient endurance on his people because the coming of the Lord is drawing near (James 5:8); soon their distress will be at an end. The writer to the Hebrews urges patience,

for soon the one that shall come will come (Hebrews 10:37).

In the New Testament, the idea of the coming of Christ was used as a warning to the heedless and as a comfort to the oppressed. It is quite true that, in the literal sense, Jesus Christ did not come back to those who were warned and exhorted in this way. But no one knows when eternity will invade life and God will bid us rise and come; and that must warn the careless to prepare to meet God and cheer the oppressed with the thought of the coming glory of the faithful soul.

There is another warning here. The risen Christ bids the Philadelphians hold to what they have, so that no one may take their crown (verse 11). It is a question not of someone stealing their crown but of God taking it from them and giving it to someone else, because they were not worthy to wear it. R. C. Trench makes a list of people in the Bible who lost their place to someone else because they had shown that they were not fit to hold it. Esau lost his place to Jacob (Genesis 25:34, 27:36). Reuben, unstable as water, lost his place to Judah (Genesis 49:4, 49:8). Saul lost his place to David (1 Samuel 16:1, 16:13). Shebna lost his place to Eliakim (Isaiah 22:15–25). Joab and Abiathar lost their places to Benaiah and Zadok (1 Kings 2:25). Judas lost his place to Matthias (Acts 1:25–6). The Jews lost their place to the Gentiles (Romans 11:11).

There is tragedy here. It sometimes happens that someone is given a task to do and goes towards it with the highest hopes; but it begins to be seen that that person is not up to the task, and it is therefore given to someone else. That can happen with the tasks of God. God has a task for each one of us; but it may be that we prove ourselves unfit for the task, and it is given to someone else.

It is blessedly true that even out of failure we can redeem ourselves – but only if we cast ourselves upon the grace of Jesus Christ.

PHILADELPHIA: MANY PROMISES

Revelation 3:7–13 (*contd*)

IN verse 12, we come to the promises of the risen Christ to those who are faithful. They are many, and most would paint pictures which would be vivid and real to the people of Philadelphia.

(1) Faithful Christians will be pillars in the Temple of God. A pillar of the Church is a great and honoured support. Peter, James and John were the pillars of the early church in Jerusalem (Galatians 2:9). Abraham, said the Jewish Rabbis, was the pillar of the world.

(2) Faithful Christians will go out no more. There may be something of two meanings here.

(a) This may be a promise of security. We have seen how, for years, Philadelphia was terrorized by recurring earthquakes and how, when such times came, its citizens fled into the open country to escape and, when the tremors ended, came uncertainly back. Life was lived in an atmosphere of insecurity. There is for faithful Christians the promise of a settled serenity in the peace which Jesus Christ can give.

(b) Some scholars think that what is promised here is firmness of moral character. In this life, even the best of us is sometimes bad. But those who are faithful will in the end come to a time when they are like a pillar fixed in the Temple of God, and goodness has become the constant atmosphere of their lives. If this is the meaning, this phrase describes the life of untroubled goodness which is lived when, after the battles of earth, we reach the presence of God.

(3) Jesus Christ will write on faithful Christians the name of their God. There may be three pictures here.

(a) In the cities of Asia Minor, and in Philadelphia, when a priest died after a lifetime of faithfulness, he was honoured by erecting a new pillar in the temple in which he had served and by inscribing his name and the name of his father upon it. This, then, would describe the lasting honour which Christ pays to his faithful ones.

(b) It is just possible that there is a reference to the custom of branding slaves with the initials of their owners to show to whom they belong. In the same way, God will put his mark upon his faithful ones. Whichever picture is behind this, the sense is that the faithful ones will wear the unmistakable badge of God.

(c) It is just possible that we have here an Old Testament picture. When God told to Moses the blessing which Aaron and the priests must pronounce over the people, he said: 'They shall put my name on the Israelites' (Numbers 6:27). It is the same idea again; it is as if the mark of God was on Israel so that all might know that they are his people.

(4) On faithful Christians, the name of the new Jerusalem is to be written. That stands for the gift to faithful Christians of citizenship in the city of God. According to Ezekiel, the name of the re-created city of God was to be *the Lord is there* (Ezekiel 48:35). The faithful ones will be citizens of the city where there is always the presence of God.

(5) On faithful Christians, Christ will write his own new name. The people of Philadelphia knew all about taking a new name. When in AD 17 a terrible earthquake devastated their city, and Tiberius, the emperor, dealt kindly with them, cancelling taxation and making a generous gift to rebuild it, in their gratitude they called the city Neocaesarea, the New City of Caesar; and later, when Vespasian was kind to them, they called it Flavia, for that was the family name of Vespasian. Jesus Christ will mark his faithful ones with his new name: what that name was, we need not even speculate, for no one knows it (Revelation 19:12); but, in the time to come, when

Christ has conquered all, his faithful ones will bear the badge which shows that they are his and share his triumph.

THE LETTER TO LAODICEA

Revelation 3:14–22

And to the angel of the church in Laodicea, write:

These things says the Amen, the witness on whom you can rely and who is true, the moving cause of the creation of God.

I know your works; I know that you are neither cold nor hot. Would that you were cold or hot! So, because you are tepid and neither cold nor hot, I will vomit you out of my mouth. Because you say, I am rich and I have acquired riches, and I need nothing, and are quite unaware that it is you who are the wretched and the pitiable one, the poor and the blind and the naked one, I advise you to buy from me gold that has been refined by fire that you may be rich, white raiment that you may be clothed and that the shame of your nakedness may not be openly displayed, and eye-salve to anoint your eyes, that you may see.

I rebuke and discipline all those whom I love. Be eager, therefore, and repent.

Behold, I am standing at the door and knocking. If anyone hears my voice and opens the door, I will come in and will have my meal with him, and he with me.

I will give to him who overcomes to sit with me in my throne, even as I also overcame and took my seat with my Father in his throne.

Let him who has an ear hear what the Spirit is saying to the churches.

LAODICEA: THE CHURCH CONDEMNED

Revelation 3:14–22 (*contd*)

LAODICEA has the grim distinction of being the only church of which the risen Christ has nothing good to say.

In the ancient world, there were at least six cities called Laodicea, and this one was called Laodicea on the Lycus to distinguish it from the others. It was founded in about 250 BC by Antiochus of Syria and was named after his wife Laodicē.

Its importance was due entirely to its position. The road from Ephesus to the east and to Syria was the most important in Asia. It began at the coast at Ephesus, and it had to find a way to climb to the central plateau 8,500 feet above. It set out along the valley of the River Maeander until it reached what were known as the Gates of Phrygia. Beyond this point lay a broad valley where Lydia, Phrygia and Caria met. The Maeander entered that valley by a narrow, precipitous gorge through which no road could pass. The road, therefore, made a detour through the Lycus valley. Laodicea stood in that valley.

It was situated literally astride the great road to the east which went straight through Laodicea, entering by the Ephesian Gate and leaving by the Syrian Gate. That in itself would have been enough to make Laodicea one of the great commercial and strategic centres of the ancient world. Originally, Laodicea had been a fortress; but it had the serious handicap that all its water supply had to come by underground aqueduct from springs no less than six miles away, a perilous situation for a besieged town. Two other roads passed through the gates of Laodicea, that from Pergamum and the Hermus valley to Pisidia and Pamphylia and the coast at Perga, and that from eastern Caria to central and west Phrygia.

As Sir William Ramsay says: 'It only needed peace to make Laodicea a great commercial and financial centre.' That peace came with the dominion of Rome. When the Roman peace gave it its opportunity, it became, as Pliny, the governor of Bithynia, called it, 'a most distinguished city'.

Laodicea had certain characteristics which have left their mark on the letter written to it.

(1) It was a great banking and financial centre. When Cicero was travelling in Asia Minor, it was at Laodicea that he cashed his letters of credit. It was one of the wealthiest cities in the world. In AD 61, it was devastated by an earthquake; but its citizens were so rich and independent that they refused any help from the Roman government and rebuilt their city out of their own resources. The Roman historian Tacitus writes: 'One of the most famous cities of Asia, Laodicea, was in that same year overthrown by an earthquake and without any relief from us recovered itself by its own resources' (*Annals*, 14:27). No wonder Laodicea could boast that it was rich and had amassed wealth and needed nothing. It was so wealthy that it did not even need God.

(2) It was a great centre for the manufacture of clothing. The sheep which grazed round Laodicea were famous for their soft, violet-black, glossy wool. The city mass-produced cheap outer garments. It was especially connected with a tunic called the *trimita* – so much so, indeed, that it was sometimes called Trimitaria. Laodicea was so proud of the garments it produced that it never realized it was naked in the sight of God.

(3) It was a very considerable medical centre. Thirteen miles to the west, between Laodicea and the Gate of Phrygia, stood the temple of the Carian god Men. At one time, that temple was the social, administrative and commercial centre of the whole area. Until the end of the nineteenth century, great markets were regularly held on its site. In particular, the temple

was the centre of a medical school which was transferred to Laodicea itself. Its doctors were so famous that the names of some appear on the coins of Laodicea. Two of them were called Zeuxis and Alexander Philalethes.

This medical school was famous throughout the world for two things – ointment for the ear and ointment for the eyes. The Authorized and Revised Standard Versions speak of eye-*salve*. The word for *salve* is *kollurion*, which literally means *a little roll of bread*. The derivation of this word is the famous *tephra Phrygia* – Phrygian powder which was exported all over the world in solidified tablet form in the shape of little rolls. Laodicea was so conscious of its medical skill in the care of the eyes that it never realized that it was spiritually blind.

The words of the risen Christ arise directly from the prosperity and the skill in which Laodicea took so much pride and which had in the minds of its citizens, and even of its church, eliminated the need for God.

(4) We add a final fact about Laodicea. It was in an area where there was a very large Jewish population. So many Jews emigrated here that the Rabbis spoke out strongly against the Jews who sought the wines and baths of Phrygia. In 62 BC, Flaccus, the governor of the province, became alarmed at the amount of currency that the Jews were exporting in payment of the Temple tax which every male Jew paid, and put an embargo on the export of currency. The result was that twenty pounds' weight of gold was seized as contraband in Laodicea and 100 pounds' weight in Apameia in Phrygia. That amount of gold would be equal to 15,000 silver drachmae. The Jewish Temple tax amounted to half a shekel, which was equal to two drachmae. This means that in the district there were at least 7,500 male Jews. In Hierapolis, six miles away from Laodicea, there was a 'Congregation of Jews' which had power to levy and to retain fines, and an archive office where Jewish legal

documents were specially kept. There can have been few areas where the Jews were wealthier and more influential.

LAODICEA: THE CLAIMS OF CHRIST

Revelation 3:14–22 (contd)

OF all the seven churches, that of Laodicea is most unsparingly condemned. In it, there is no redeeming feature. It is interesting to note that the third-century work *The Apostolic Constitutions* (8:46) says that Archippus was the first bishop of the church in Laodicea. When Paul is writing to the neighbouring church of Colosse, he says sternly: 'And say to Archippus, "See that you complete the task that you have received in the Lord"' (Colossians 4:17). It would seem that Archippus was somehow failing in his duty. That was thirty years before Revelation was written; but it may be that in the church in Laodicea the rot had set in as long ago as that, and an unsatisfactory ministry had sown the seeds of degeneration.

Like all the letters, it begins with a series of titles of Jesus Christ.

(1) He is the Amen. This is a strange title and has two possible origins.

(a) In Isaiah 65:16, God is called the God of faithfulness; but in the Hebrew he is called the *God of Amen*. Amen is the word which is often put at the end of a solemn statement in order to guarantee its truth. If God is the God of Amen, he is utterly to be relied upon. This would mean that Jesus Christ is the one whose promises are true beyond all doubt.

(b) In John's gospel, Jesus' statements often begin: 'Very truly, I tell you' (e.g. John 1:51, 3:3, 3:5, 3:11). The Greek for *truly* is *Amen*. It is possible that, when Jesus Christ is called the Amen, it is a reminiscence of his own way of speaking.

The meaning would be the same as for the previous derivation; Jesus is one whose promises can be relied upon.

(2) He is the witness on whom we can rely and who is true. R. C. Trench points out that witnesses must satisfy three essential conditions. (a) They must have seen with their own eyes what they report on. (b) They must be absolutely honest, so that they repeat with accuracy what they have heard and seen. (c) They must have the ability to communicate what they have to say, so that their testimony may make its true impression on those who hear. Jesus Christ perfectly satisfied these conditions. He can speak about God, because he came from him. We can rely on his words, for he is the Amen. He is able to communicate his message, for no one ever spoke as he did.

(3) As the Revised Standard Version has it, he is the beginning of God's creation. This phrase, as it stands in English, is ambiguous. It could mean either that Jesus was the first person to be created or that he began the process of creation – as Trench put it, 'dynamically the beginning'. It is the second meaning which is intended here. The word for *beginning* is *archē*. In early Christian writings, we read that Satan is the *archē* of death, that is to say, death takes its origin in him; and that God is the *archē* of all things, that is, all things find their beginning in him.

The connection of the Son with creation is frequently made in the New Testament. John begins his gospel by saying of the word: 'All things came into being through him, and without him not one thing came into being' (John 1:3). 'In him,' says Paul, 'all things ... were created' (Colossians 1:16). The insistence on the Son's part in creation was due to the heretics who explained sin and disease by saying that the world had been created by a false and inferior god. It is the Christian insistence that this world is God's creation and that its sin and sorrow are not his fault but are caused by the disobedience of men and women. As Christians see it, the God of creation and the God of redemption are one and the same.

LAODICEA: NEITHER ONE THING NOR ANOTHER

Revelation 3:14–22 (contd)

THE condemnation of Laodicea begins with a picture of almost crude vividness; because the Laodiceans are neither cold nor hot, they have about them a kind of nauseating quality, which will make the risen Christ vomit them out of his mouth.

The exact meaning of the words is to be noted. *Cold* is *psuchros*, and it can mean cold to the point of freezing. Sirach ([Ecclesiasticus] 43:20) speaks of the *cold* north wind, which makes the ice freeze upon the waters. *Hot* is *zestos*, and it means hot to boiling point. *Tepid* is *chliaros*. Things which are tepid often have a nauseating effect. Hot food and cold food can both be appetising, but tepid food will often make us feel sick. Directly opposite Laodicea, on the other bank of the Lycus, and in full view, stood Hierapolis, famous for its hot mineral springs. Often, hot mineral springs are nauseating in their taste and make the person who drinks them want to be physically sick. That is the way in which the church at Laodicea affected the risen Christ. Here is something to make us think.

(1) The one attitude which the risen Christ unsparingly condemns is indifference. It has been said that it is possible to write a good biography if the author loves or hates the subject, but not if there is only a feeling of cold indifference. Of all things, indifference is the hardest to combat. The problem of modern evangelism is not hostility to Christianity; it would be better if it were so. The problem is that, to so many, Christianity and the

Church have ceased to have any relevance, and people regard them with complete indifference. This indifference can be broken down only by the actual demonstration that Christianity is a power to make life strong and a grace to make life beautiful.

(2) The one impossible attitude to Christianity is neutrality. Jesus Christ works through individuals; and those who remain completely detached in their attitude to him have by that very fact refused to undertake the work which is the divine purpose for them. Those who will not submit to Christ have therefore resisted him.

(3) Hard as it may sound, the meaning of this terrible threat from the risen Christ is that it is better not even to start on the Christian way than to start and then to drift into a conventional and meaningless Christianity. The fire must be kept burning. There is an unwritten saying of Jesus: 'The one who is near me is near the fire.' And the way to 'maintain the spiritual glow' (Romans 12:11, Moffatt's translation) is to live close to Christ.

LAODICEA: THE WEALTH THAT IS POVERTY

Revelation 3:14–22 (*contd*)

THE tragedy of Laodicea was that it was convinced of its own wealth and blind to its own poverty. Humanly speaking, anyone would say that there was not a more prosperous town in Asia Minor. Spiritually speaking, the risen Christ declares that there was not a more poverty-stricken community. Laodicea prided itself on three things; and each is taken in turn and shown at its true value.

(1) It prided itself on its financial wealth. It was rich and had acquired wealth and needed nothing – or so it thought. The risen Christ advises Laodicea to buy gold refined in the

fire. It may be that gold tested in the fire stands for faith, for Peter describes faith in this way (1 Peter 1:7). Wealth can do much, but there are things that it can never do. It cannot buy happiness or give us health either of body or of mind; it cannot bring comfort in sorrow or fellowship in loneliness. If all that we have to meet life with is wealth, we are poor indeed. But if we have a faith tried and refined through experience, there is nothing which we cannot face; and we are rich indeed.

(2) Laodicea prided itself on its clothing trade. The garments made there were famous all the world over, and the wool of the sheep of Laodicea was a universally recognized luxury article. But, says the risen Christ, Laodicea is spiritually naked; if it wants really to be clothed, it must come to him. The risen Christ speaks of 'the shame of your nakedness'.

This would mean even more in the ancient world than now. In the ancient world, to be stripped naked was the worst humiliation. Hanum treated the servants of David in this way (2 Samuel 10:4). The threat to Egypt is that Assyria will lead its people naked and barefoot (Isaiah 20:4). It was Ezekiel's threat to Israel that its enemies would strip away its clothes (Ezekiel 16:37–9, 23:26–9; cf. Hosea 2:3, 2:9; Micah 1:8, 1:11). God's threat passed on by Nahum to the disobedient people was: 'I will let nations look on your nakedness, and kingdoms on your shame' (Nahum 3:5). On the other hand, to be dressed in fine clothes was the greatest honour. Pharaoh honoured Joseph by clothing him in garments of fine linen (Genesis 41:42). Daniel is clothed in purple by Belshazzar (Daniel 5:29). The royal apparel is for the one whom the king honours (Esther 6:6–11). When the prodigal son returns, it is the best robe that is put upon him (Luke 15:22).

Laodicea prides itself on the magnificent garments it produces; but spiritually it is naked, and nakedness means shame. The risen Christ urges it to buy white robes from him.

This may well stand for the beauties of life and character which only the grace of Christ can give. There is little point in adorning the body if we have nothing with which to adorn the soul. All the clothes in the world will never bring beauty to a person whose nature is twisted and whose character is ugly.

(3) Laodicea prided itself on its famous eye-salve; but the facts show that it was blind to its own poverty and nakedness. Trench says: 'The beginning of all true amendment is to see ourselves as we are.' All eye-salves in the ancient world caused the eyes to smart when first applied; and Laodicea had no wish to see itself as it was.

LAODICEA: DISCIPLINED OUT OF LOVE

Revelation 3:14–22 (contd)

VERSE 19 is one which expresses teaching that runs throughout Scripture: 'I rebuke and discipline all those whom I love.' There is a very lovely thing about the way this is put. It is a quotation from Proverbs 3:12, but one word is altered. In the Greek of the Septuagint, the word for *love* is *agapan*, which indicates the unconquerable attitude of goodwill which nothing can turn to hate; but it is a word which maybe has more of the head than the heart in it; and, in the quotation, the risen Christ changes *agapan* to *philein*, which is the most tender affection. We might well paraphrase it: 'It is the people who are dearest to me on whom I exercise the sternest discipline.'

Let us first take the word *rebuke*. The Greek is *elegchein*, and it describes the kind of rebuke which compels people to see the error of their ways. *Elegchos* is the corresponding noun, and Aristotle defines it: '*Elegchos* is the proof that a thing cannot be otherwise than we say.' The most vivid example of this kind of rebuke is the way in which Nathan opened David's

eyes to his sin (2 Samuel 12:1–14). The rebuke of God is not
so much punishment as illumination.

Let us see how the idea of discipline runs through the
Bible.

It is very characteristic of the teaching of Proverbs. 'Those
who spare the rod hate their children, but those who love them
are diligent to discipline them' (Proverbs 13:24). 'Do not
withhold discipline from your children; if you beat them with
a rod, they will not die. If you beat them with the rod, you will
save their lives from Sheol' (Proverbs 23:13–14). 'Well meant
are the wounds a friend inflicts' (Proverbs 27:6). 'The rod and
reproof give wisdom, but a mother is disgraced by a neglected
child ... Discipline your children, and they will give you rest;
they will give delight to your heart' (Proverbs 29:15, 29:17).
'Happy are those whom you discipline, O Lord, and whom you
teach out of your law' (Psalm 94:12). 'How happy is the one
whom God reproves; therefore do not despise the discipline
of the Almighty' (Job 5:17). 'We are disciplined [by the Lord]
so that we may not be condemned along with the world'
(1 Corinthians 11:32). 'For the Lord disciplines those whom
he loves, and chastises every child whom he accepts. Endure
trials for the sake of discipline. God is treating you as children;
for what child is there whom a parent does not discipline? If
you do not have that discipline in which all children share, then
you are illegitimate and not his children' (Hebrews 11:6–8).
'He who loves his son will whip him often, so that he may
rejoice in the way he turns out. He who disciplines his son will
profit by him, and will boast about him among acquaintances'
(Sirach [Ecclesiasticus] 30:1).

It is, in fact, God's final punishment to leave someone alone.
'Ephraim is joined to idols – let him alone' (Hosea 4:17). As
R. C. Trench has it: 'The great Master-builder squares and
polishes with many strokes of the chisel and hammer the stones

which shall find a place at last in the walls of the heavenly Jerusalem ... It is the crushed grape, and not the untouched, from which the costly liquor distils.' There is no surer way of allowing children to come to grief than to allow them to do as they like. It is a fact of life that the best athletes and the finest scholars receive the most demanding training. The discipline of God is not something which we should resent, but something for which we should be devoutly thankful.

LAODICEA: THE CHRIST WHO KNOCKS

Revelation 3:14–22 (contd)

IN verse 20, we have one of the most famous pictures of Jesus in the whole New Testament. 'Behold,' says the risen Christ, 'I am standing at the door and knocking.' This picture has been derived from two different sources.

(1) It has been taken as a warning that the end is near, and that the coming of Christ is at hand. Christians must be ready to open whenever they hear their Lord knocking (Luke 12:36). When the signs come, Christians will know that the end time is near, even at the door (Mark 13:29; Matthew 24:33). Christians must live well and live in love because the judge is standing at the doors (James 5:9). It is true that the New Testament uses this picture to express the imminence of the coming of Christ. If that is the picture here, this phrase contains a warning and tells people to take care, for Jesus Christ the Judge and King is at the door.

(2) We cannot say that that meaning is impossible – and yet it does not seem to fit the context, for the atmosphere of the passage is not so much warning as love. It is much better to take this saying of Christ as expressing the appeal of the one who loves the souls of men and women. The origin of the

passage is much more likely to be in the Song of Solomon, when the lover stands outside and pleads with his beloved to open the door. 'Listen! my beloved is knocking. "Open to me, my sister, my love, my dove, my perfect one"' (Song of Solomon 5:2–6). Here is Christ the lover knocking at the door of human hearts. And in this picture we see certain great truths of Christianity.

(a) We see the pleading of Christ. He stands at the door of the human heart and knocks. The unique new fact that Christianity brought into this world is that God is the one who seeks for people. No other religion has the vision of a seeking God.

In his book, *Out of Nazareth*, Donald Baillie cites three witnesses to the uniqueness of this idea. C. J. G. Montefiore, the great Jewish scholar, said that the one thing which no Jewish prophet or Rabbi ever imagined is the 'conception of God actually going out in quest of sinful men, who were not seeking him, but who were turned away from him'. A document produced by the National Christian Council of Japan describes the distinctive difference of Christianity from all other religions as being found in 'Man not seeking God, but God taking the initiative in seeking man'. Way back in the twelfth century, St Bernard often used to say to his monks that 'However early they might wake and rise for prayer in their chapel on a cold mid-winter morning, or even in the dead of night, they would always find God awake before them, waiting for them – nay, it was he who had awakened them to seek his face.'

Here is the picture of Christ searching for sinful men and women who did not want him. Surely love can go no further than that.

(b) We see the offer of Christ. As the Authorized Version has it, 'I will come in and sup with him.' The word translated as *sup* is *deipnein*, and its corresponding noun is *deipnon*. The Greeks had three meals in the day. There was *akratisma*, breakfast, which was no more than a piece of dried bread dipped in wine. There was *ariston*, the midday meal. People did not go home for it; it was simply a picnic snack eaten by the side of the pavement, or in some colonnade, or in the city square. There was *deipnon*; this was the evening meal, the main meal of the day, and people lingered over it, for the day's work was done. It was the *deipnon* that Christ would share with those who answered his knock – no hurried meal, but a meal where people lingered in fellowship. If people will open the door, Jesus Christ will come in and spend time with them.

(3) We see human responsibility. Christ knocks, and people can answer or refuse to answer. Christ does not break in; he must be invited in. Even on the Emmaus road, 'He walked ahead as if he were going on' (Luke 24:28). Holman Hunt was right when, in his famous picture *The Light of the World*, he painted the door of the human heart with no handle on the outside, for it can be opened only from the inside. As Trench has it: 'Every man is lord of the house of his own heart; it is his fortress; he must open the gates of it'; and he has 'the mournful prerogative and privilege of refusing to open'. The one who refuses to open is 'blindly at strife with his own blessedness' – a 'miserable conqueror'.

Christ pleads and offers; but it is all to no avail if we will not open the door.

THIS MEANS YOU

Revelation 3:14–22 (*contd*)

THE promise of the risen Christ is that the victor will sit with him in his own victorious throne. We will get the picture right if we remember that the eastern throne was more like a couch than a single seat. The victor in life will share the throne of the victorious Christ.

Every letter finishes with the words: 'Let anyone who has an ear hear what the Spirit is saying to the churches.' This saying does two things.

(1) It individualizes the message of the letters. It says to every single person: 'This means you.' So often, we listen to a message which comes through a preacher and apply it to everyone but ourselves. In our heart of hearts, we believe that the stern words cannot possibly be meant for us and that the promises are too good to be true for us. This phrase says to each one of us: 'All these things are meant for *you*.'

(2) It generalizes the message of the letters. It means that their message was not confined to the people in the seven churches nearly 2,000 years ago, but that through them the Spirit is speaking to every individual in every generation. We have set these letters carefully against the local situations to which they were addressed; but their message is not local and temporary. It is eternal, and in them the Spirit still speaks to us.

THE OPENING HEAVENS AND THE OPENING DOOR

Revelation 4:1

> After this I saw, and, behold, a door in heaven was stand-
> ing open, and there came to me the voice that I had heard
> before, speaking to me like the sound of a trumpet, and
> the speaker said: 'Come up here, and I will show you the
> events which must follow these things.'

IN chapters 2–3, we saw the risen Christ walking among his churches upon earth. Now the scene changes to the court of heaven.

A door was opened in heaven for the seer. There are two possibilities here. (1) It may be that he is thought of as already being in heaven, and the door is opening into even more holy parts of heaven. (2) It is much more likely that the door is from earth to heaven. Primitive Jewish thought pictured the sky as a vast solid dome, set like a roof upon a square flat earth; and the idea here is that beyond the dome of the sky there is heaven, and a door is opened in that dome to give the seer entry into heaven.

In the early chapters of Revelation, there are three of the most important doors in life.

(1) There is *the door of opportunity*. 'Look,' said the risen Christ to the church at Philadelphia, 'I have set before you an open door' (Revelation 3:8). That was the door of the glorious opportunity by which the message of the gospel could be taken to the regions beyond. God sets before every one of us our own door of opportunity.

(2) There is *the door of the human heart*. 'Listen!' says the risen Christ, 'I am standing at the door, knocking' (Revelation 3:20). At the door of every heart there comes the knock of the nail-pierced hand, and we may open or refuse to open.

(3) There is *the door of revelation*. 'I looked, and there in heaven a door stood open,' says the seer. God offers to every one of us the door which leads to the knowledge of God and of life eternal.

More than once, the New Testament speaks of the heavens *being opened*; and it is of the greatest significance to see the object of that opening.

(1) There is the opening of the heavens for *vision*. 'The heavens were opened, and I saw visions of God' (Ezekiel 1:1). God sends to those who seek him the vision of himself and of his truth.

(2) There is the opening for *the descent of the Spirit*. When Jesus was baptized by John, he saw the heavens opened and the Spirit descending upon himself (Mark 1:10). When our minds and souls seek upwards, the Spirit of God descends to meet them.

(3) There is the opening for *the revelation of the glory of Christ*. It was the promise of Jesus to Nathanael that he would see the heaven open and the angels of God ascending and descending upon the Son of Man (John 1:51). Some day, the heavens will open to disclose the glory of Christ; and inevitably that day will bring joy to those who have loved him and amazement and fear to those who have despised him.

THE THRONE OF GOD

Revelation 4:2-3

> Immediately, I fell under the influence of the Spirit; and, behold, a throne stood in heaven, and there was one seated on it. And he who was seated on the throne was like a jasper stone and a sardian to look at; and there was a rainbow circling round the throne, like an emerald to look at.

WHEN the seer entered the door into heaven, he fell into an ecstasy.

In heaven, he saw a throne and God on the throne. The throne of God is a common Old Testament picture. The prophet said: 'I saw the Lord sitting on his throne, with all the host of heaven standing beside him' (1 Kings 22:19). The psalmist has it: 'God sits on his holy throne' (Psalm 47:8). Isaiah saw the Lord 'sitting on a throne, high and lofty' (Isaiah 6:1). In Revelation, the throne of God is mentioned in every chapter except chapters 2, 8 and 9. The throne of God stands for the majesty of God. When Handel was asked how he had come to write the *Messiah*, his answer was: 'I saw the heavens opened and God upon his great white throne.'

John saw one seated on the throne. There is something very interesting here. John makes no attempt to describe God in any human shape. As H. B. Swete says, 'He rigorously shuns anthropomorphic details.' He describes God in 'the flashing of gem-like colours', but he never mentions any kind of form. It is a familiar theme in the Bible to see God in terms of light. The Pastoral Epistles describe God as dwelling in 'unapproachable light' (1 Timothy 6:16). And, long before that, the psalmist had spoken of God who wraps himself with light as with a garment (Psalm 104:2).

John sees his vision in terms of the lights which flash from precious stones. We do not know what exactly these stones were. The three names here are jasper, sardian and emerald. One thing is certain: these were typical of the most precious stones. Plato mentions the three of them together as representative of precious stones (*Phaedo*, 111 E). They were part of the rich array of the King of Tyre (Ezekiel 28:13); they were among the precious stones on the breastplate of the high priest (Exodus 28:17); and they were among the stones which were the foundation of the holy city (Revelation 21:19).

The *jasper* is nowadays a dull opaque stone, but in the ancient world it seems to have been a translucent rock crystal, through which the light would come with an almost unbearable brilliance. Some think that here it means a diamond – and this is not impossible. The *sardian*, so called because it was said to be found mainly near Sardis, was blood-red; it was a gem which frequently used to have engravings incised on it and may correspond to the modern carnelian. The *emerald* is most likely the green emerald which we know.

The picture of the presence of God which John saw was like the blinding flash of a diamond in the sun, with the dazzling blood-red of the sardian; and there flashed through both the more restful green of the emerald, for only in that way could the eye bear to look upon the sight.

It may well be that the *jasper* stands for the unbearable brightness of the *purity* of God; that the blood-red *sardian* stands for his avenging *wrath*; and that the gentle green of the *emerald* stands for his *mercy*, by which alone we can meet his purity and his justice.

THE TWENTY-FOUR ELDERS

Revelation 4:4

> And in a circle round the throne I saw twenty-four thrones, and seated upon the thrones twenty-four elders, clothed in white garments, with golden crowns upon their heads.

WE now approach one of the difficult passages for which Revelation is notorious. In it, we meet twenty-four elders and then four living creatures; and we have to try to identify them.

We find the twenty-four elders frequently appearing in Revelation. Let us set down the facts about them. They sit around the throne, clothed in white robes and wearing crowns (4:4, 14:3); they cast their crowns before the throne (4:10); they continually worship and praise (5:11, 5:14, 7:11, 11:16, 14:3, 19:4); they bring to God the prayers of the saints (5:8); one of them encourages the seer, when he is sad (5:5); and one of them acts as interpreter of one of the visions (7:13). We may note five lines of explanation.

(1) In the Old Testament, there are indications of a kind of council surrounding God. The prophet sees God sitting on

his throne and all the host of heaven standing by him on his right hand and on his left (1 Kings 22:19). In Job, the sons of God come to meet with him (Job 1:6, 2:1). Isaiah speaks of God reigning in glory among his elders (Isaiah 24:23). In the Genesis story of the garden, the accusation against Adam is that he has eaten of the fruit of the forbidden tree and become like one of *us* (Genesis 3:22). It may be that the idea of the elders has something to do with the idea of God's council surrounding him.

(2) When the Jews were in Babylon, they could not avoid coming into contact with Babylonian ideas. And it might well be that sometimes they incorporated Babylonian ideas into their own thinking, especially if there was some initial resemblance. The Babylonians had twenty-four star gods, for the worship of the stars was a part of Babylonian religion; and it has been suggested that these became, in Jewish thought, twenty-four angels who surrounded the throne of God, and that the elders stand for these.

(3) We move on to explanations which we think are much more likely. There were so many priests in Israel that they could not possibly serve in the Temple at the one time, and so they were divided into twenty-four different courses (1 Chronicles 24:7–18). Each of these courses had its president, known as an elder of the priests. Sometimes these elders were called officers, or governors, of the house of God (1 Chronicles 24:5). It is suggested that the twenty-four elders stand symbolically for the twenty-four courses of the priests. They present the prayers of the faithful to God (Revelation 5:8), and that is priestly work. The Levites were similarly divided into twenty-four courses for the work of the Temple, and they praised God with harps and lyres and cymbals (1 Chronicles 25:6–31); and the elders also have their harps (Revelation 5:8). So the twenty-four elders may stand for the

heavenly ideal of the earthly worship of the priests and Levites in the Temple.

(4) It has been suggested that the twenty-four elders stand for the twelve patriarchs and the twelve apostles combined. In the new Jerusalem, the names of the twelve patriarchs are on the twelve gates and the names of the twelve apostles are on the foundation stones of the wall.

(5) We think that the most likely explanation is that the twenty-four elders are the symbolic representatives of the faithful people of God. Their white robes are the robes promised to the faithful (Revelation 3:4), and their crowns (*stephanoi*) are those promised to those who are faithful even to death (Revelation 2:10). The thrones are those which Jesus promised to those who forsook all and followed him (Matthew 19:27–9). The description of the twenty-four elders fits well with the promises made to the faithful.

The question will then be: 'Why twenty-four?' The answer is because the Church is composed of Jews *and* Gentiles. There were originally twelve tribes, but now it is as if the tribes were doubled. Swete says that the twenty-four elders stand for the Church *in its totality*. We remember that this is a vision not of what yet is but of what shall be; and the twenty-four elders stand as representatives of the whole Church which one day in glory will worship in the presence of God himself.

AROUND THE THRONE

Revelation 4:5–6a

> And flashes of lightning and voices and peals of thunder were coming forth from the throne. There were seven torches of fire burning before the throne, and these are the seven Spirits of God. And in front of the throne there was what I can only call a sea of glass like crystal.

JOHN adds more details to his mysterious and awe-inspiring picture of heaven. The voices are the voices of the thunder; and thunder and lightning are often connected with the manifestation of God. In the vision of Ezekiel, lightning comes out of the fiery haze around the throne (Ezekiel 1:13). The psalmist tells how the voice of the thunder of God was heard in the heavens, and the lightnings lit up the world (Psalm 77:18). God sends his lightning to the ends of the earth (Job 37:4). But what is primarily in the mind of John is the description of Mount Sinai as the people waited for the giving of the law: 'There was thunder and lightning, as well as a thick cloud on the mountain, and a blast of a trumpet so loud that all the people who were in the camp trembled' (Exodus 19:16). John is using imagery which is regularly connected with the presence of God.

The seven torches are the seven Spirits of God. We have already met the seven Spirits before the throne (Revelation 1:4, 3:1). There are scholars who see Babylonian influence here also. For the Babylonians, the seven planets were also divine and within the presence of God; it would be natural to liken the planets to torches, and it has been suggested that this imagery is Babylonian in origin.

The 'glassy sea' has exercised a strange fascination over the minds of many people, including hymn-writers. The Greek does not say that there was a sea of glass but 'as it were a sea of glass'. There was something which was beyond all description, but which could be likened only to a great sea of glass. Where did the seer get this picture?

(1) He may have got it from an idea in the most primitive thought of the Old Testament. We have already seen that the firmament is conceived of as a great solid dome arching over the earth. Beneath it is the earth, and above it the heaven. The creation story speaks of the waters under the firmament and

the waters *above* the firmament (Genesis 1:7). The psalmist calls upon the waters that are above the heavens to praise the Lord (Psalm 148:4). The belief was that above the firmament, perhaps as the kind of floor of heaven, there was a great sea. Further, it was on that sea that God had set his throne. The psalmist says of God that he set the beams of his chambers upon the waters (Psalm 104:3).

(2) It may be that John's time in Patmos gave him the idea for this picture. Swete suggests that he saw a vast surface which reflected the light, 'like the Aegean Sea, when on summer days John looked upon it from the heights of Patmos'. John had often seen the sea like a sea of molten glass, and maybe his picture was born from that.

(3) There is a further possibility. According to the Qur'an (Sura 27), Solomon had in his palace a floor of glass so like a sea that, when the Queen of Sheba came to visit him, she picked up her skirts thinking she had to wade through water. It may be that John is thinking of the throne of God set in a glass-floored palace.

(4) There is one other remote possibility. John says that the glassy sea was like *crystal* (*krustallon*); but *krustallon* could mean *ice*; and then the idea would be an expanse which shimmered like an ice-field. It is a magnificent picture; but it can hardly be the real picture, because neither John nor his people would ever have seen such a scene, and it would have meant nothing to them.

There are three things that this sea like shining glass does symbolize.

(1) It symbolizes *preciousness*. In the ancient world, glass was usually dull and semi-opaque, and glass as clear as crystal was as precious as gold. In Job 28:17, gold and glass are mentioned together as examples of precious things.

(2) It symbolizes *dazzling purity*. The blinding light reflected from the glassy sea would be too much for the eyes to look upon, like the purity of God.

(3) It symbolizes *immense distance*. The throne of God was in the far distance, as if at the other side of a great sea. Swete writes of 'the vast distance which, even in the case of one who stood in the door of heaven, intervened between himself and the throne of God'.

One of the greatest characteristics of the writing of the seer is the reverence which, even in the heavenly places, never dares to be familiar with God, but paints its picture in terms of light and distance.

THE FOUR LIVING CREATURES (1)

Revelation 4:6b–8

> And, between the throne and the elders, in a circle round the throne, were four living creatures, full of eyes in front and behind. The first living creature was like a lion; the second living creature was like an ox; the third living creature had what appeared to be a man's face; the fourth living creature was like an eagle in flight. The four living creatures had each of them six wings; and around and within they were full of eyes. Night and day they never rested from saying:
>
> > Holy, holy, holy is the Lord, the Almighty,
> > who was, and who is, and who is to come.

HERE we come to another of the symbolic problems of Revelation. The four living creatures appear frequently in the heavenly scene – so let us begin by collecting what Revelation itself says about them. They are always found near the throne and the Lamb (4:6, 5:6, 14:4). They have six wings and they are full of eyes (4:6, 4:8). They are constantly engaged in praising and in worshipping God (4:8, 5:9, 5:14, 7:11, 19:4). They have certain functions to perform. They invite the dreadful manifestations of the wrath of God to appear upon the scene (6:1, 6:7). One of them hands over the bowls full of the wrath of God (15:7).

Although there are definite differences, there can be little doubt that we find the ancestors of these living creatures in the visions of Ezekiel. In Ezekiel's vision, the four living creatures each have four faces – the faces of a man, a lion, an ox and an eagle; and they support the firmament (Ezekiel 1:6, 1:10, 1:22, 1:26); the rims of the wheels are full of eyes (Ezekiel 1:18). In Ezekiel, we have all the details of the picture in Revelation, although the details are differently allocated and arranged. In spite of the differences, the family resemblance is clear.

In Ezekiel, the four living creatures are definitely identified with the *cherubim*. (It is to be noted that *-im* is the Hebrew plural ending; *cherubim* is simply *cherubs*, and *seraphim* is simply *seraphs*.) The identification is made in Ezekiel 10:20 and 10:22. The cherubim were part of the decoration of Solomon's Temple, in the place of prayer and on the walls (1 Kings 6:23–30; 2 Chronicles 3:7). They were represented on the hanging veil which shut off the Holy of Holies from the Holy Place (Exodus 26:31). There were two cherubim on the lid of the ark, called the mercy-seat; and they were so placed that they faced each other and their wings swept over to form a kind of canopy over the mercy-seat (Exodus 25:18–21). One of the most common pictures of God is sitting between the cherubim, and it is in this way that he is often addressed in prayer (2 Kings 19:15; Psalm 80:1, 99:1; Isaiah 37:16). God is represented as flying on the cherubim and on the wings of the wind (Psalm 18:10). It is the cherubim who guard the way to the garden when Adam and Eve have been banished from it (Genesis 3:24). In the later books written between the Testaments, such as the Book of Enoch, the cherubim are the guardians of the throne of God (1 Enoch 71:7).

From all this, one thing emerges clearly: the cherubim are angelic beings who are close to God and the guardians of his throne.

THE FOUR LIVING CREATURES (2)

Revelation 4:6b–8 (*contd*)

WHAT do these four living creatures symbolize?

(1) These figures are clearly part of the imagery of heaven; they are not the creation of the writer of Revelation, but are inherited from previous pictures. They may originally have come from Babylonian sources, and they may have stood for the four principal signs of the Zodiac and for the four winds coming from the four quarters of heaven. But the John who wrote Revelation was not aware of that, and he used them simply as part of the imagery of heaven in which he had been brought up.

(2) How did John himself think of the symbolism of these living creatures? We think that Swete offers the right explanation. The four living creatures stand for everything that is noblest, strongest, wisest and swiftest in nature. Each creature has the pre-eminence in its own particular sphere. The lion is supreme among beasts; the ox is supreme among cattle; the eagle is supreme among birds; and a human being is supreme among all creatures. The beasts represent all the greatness and the strength and the beauty of nature; here we see nature praising God. In the verses to follow, we see the twenty-four elders praising God; and, when we put the two pictures together, we get the picture of both nature and

humanity engaged in constant adoration of God. 'The ceaseless activity of nature under the hand of God is a ceaseless tribute of praise.'

The idea of nature praising God is one which occurs in the Old Testament more than once. 'The heavens are telling the glory of God; and the firmament proclaims his handiwork. Day to day pours forth speech, and night to night declares knowledge' (Psalm 19:1–2). 'Bless the Lord, all his works, in all places of his dominion' (Psalm 103:22). Psalm 148 is a magnificent summons to the whole of nature to join in praising God.

There is a tremendous truth here. The basic idea behind this is that anything which is fulfilling the function for which it was created is praising God. One of the basic beliefs of Stoicism was that in everything there was a spark of God, *scintilla*. 'God', said Seneca, 'is near you, with you, within you; a holy spirit sits within us.' As the classical scholar Gilbert Murray points out, the sceptics laughed at this and sought to make a fool of the whole idea. 'What,' said the sceptic, 'God in worms? God in dung beetles?' 'Why not?' demanded the Stoics. 'Cannot an earthworm serve God? Do you suppose that it is only a general who is a good soldier? Cannot those who are the lowest in rank fight their best? Happy are you, if you are serving God and carrying out his purpose as faithfully as an earthworm. Whatever carries out the function for which it was created is thereby worshipping God.'

This is a thought which opens out the most magnificent mental pictures. The humblest and the most unseen activity in the world can be the true worship of God. Work and worship literally become one. Our chief end is to glorify God and to enjoy him forever; and we carry out that function when we do what God sent us into the world to do. Work well done rises like a hymn of praise to God.

This means that doctors on their rounds, scientists in their laboratories, teachers in their classrooms, musicians making their music, artists at their canvases, shop assistants at their counters, office workers at their computers, housewives in their homes – all who are doing the work of the world as it should be done – are joining in a great act of worship.

THE SYMBOLISM OF THE LIVING CREATURES

Revelation 4:6b–8 (*contd*)

It was not long before the early Church found certain symbolisms in the living creatures, in particular of the four gospels – a representation which is often to be found in stained-glass windows in churches.

The earliest and the fullest identification was made by the Bishop of Lyons, Irenaeus, in about AD 170. He held that the four living creatures represented four aspects of the work of Jesus Christ, which in turn are represented in the four gospels.

The *lion* symbolizes the powerful and effective working of the Son of God, his leadership and his royal power. The *ox* signifies the priestly side of his work, for it is the animal of sacrifice. The *human being* symbolizes his incarnation. The *eagle* represents the gift of the Holy Spirit, hovering with his wings over the Church. John represents 'the original, effective and glorious generation of the Son from the Father', and tells how all things were made by him; and is, therefore, symbolized by the lion. Luke begins with the picture of Zacharias the priest, and tells the story of the fatted calf killed for the finding of the younger son; and is, therefore, symbolized by the ox. Matthew begins by giving us the human descent of Jesus, and 'The character of a humble and meek man is kept up throughout the whole gospel'; and is, therefore, symbolized by the human being. Mark begins with a reference to the Spirit of prophecy coming down from on high upon men and women which 'points to the winged aspect of the gospel'; and is, therefore, symbolized by the eagle.

Irenaeus goes on to say that the fourfold form of the beasts represents the four principal covenants which God made with the human race. The first was made with Adam, prior to the flood. The second was made with Noah, after the flood. The third consisted of the giving of the law to Moses. The fourth is that which restores men and women in Christ, 'raising and bearing men upon its wings into the heavenly kingdom'.

But, as we have said, there was a variety of different identifications.

The scheme of Athanasius, the fourth-century Bishop of Alexandria, was:

Matthew = the human being   Mark = the ox
Luke = the lion   John = the eagle

The scheme of Victorinus, another fourth-century theologian, was:

Matthew = the human being   Mark = the lion
Luke = the ox   John = the eagle

The scheme of Augustine, who became Bishop of Hippo at the end of the fourth century, was:

Matthew = the lion   Mark = the human being
Luke = the ox   John = the eagle

It may be said that, on the whole, Augustine's identifications became the most commonly accepted, because they fit the facts. Matthew is best represented by the lion, because in it Jesus is depicted as the Lion of Judah, the one in whom all the expectations of the prophets came true. Mark is best represented by the human being, because it is the nearest approach to a factual report of the human life of Jesus. Luke is best represented by the ox, because it depicts Jesus as the sacrifice for all classes and conditions of men and women everywhere. John is best represented by the eagle, because of all birds it flies highest and is said to be the only living creature which can look straight into the sun; and John, of all the gospels, reaches the highest heights of thought.

THE SONG OF PRAISE

Revelation 4:6b–8 (*contd*)

NIGHT and day, the living creatures never rested from their doxology of praise:

> Holy, holy, holy is the Lord, the Almighty,
> who was, and who is, and who is to come.

Here is set out the sleepless praise of nature. 'Man rests on the Sabbath, and in sleep, and in the end in death, but the course of nature is unbroken and unbroken in praise.' There is never any time when the world God made is not praising him. As John Ellerton's hymn, 'The Day Thou Gavest Lord is Ended', has it:

> As o'er each continent and island
> The dawn leads on another day,
> The voice of prayer is never silent,
> Nor dies the strain of praise away.

The doxology seizes on three aspects of God.

(1) It praises him for *his holiness* (cf. Isaiah 6:3). Again and again, we have seen that the basic idea of holiness is

difference. That is supremely true of God. He is different from human beings. That is precisely the reason why we are moved to adoration of God. If he were simply a glorified human person, we could not praise. As the poet had it: 'How could I praise, if such as I could understand?' The very mystery of God moves us to awed admiration in his presence and to amazed love that that greatness should stoop so low for us and for our salvation.

(2) It praises *his omnipotence*. God is the Almighty. The people to whom Revelation was written are under the threat of the Roman Empire, a power which no individual or nation had ever successfully withstood. Think what it must have meant to be sure that behind them stood the Almighty. The very giving of that name to God affirms the certainty of the safety of Christians – a safety which did not mean release from trouble but which made people secure in life and in death.

(3) It praises *his everlastingness*. Empires might come and empires might go; God lasts forever. Here is the triumphant affirmation that God endures unchanging amid the enmity and the rebellion of human beings.

GOD, THE LORD AND CREATOR

Revelation 4:9–11

> When the living creatures shall give glory and honour and thanksgiving to him who is seated on the throne and who lives forever and ever, the twenty-four elders shall fall down before him who is seated on the throne, and worship him who lives forever and ever, and cast their crowns before the throne, and say:
>
> It is right, our Lord and God, that you should receive the glory and the honour and the power, for you have

> created all things, and through your will all things
> exist and have been created.

HERE is the other section of the choir of thanksgiving. We have seen that the living creatures stand for nature in all its greatness and the twenty-four elders for the great united Church in Jesus Christ. So, when the living creatures and the elders unite in praise, it symbolizes nature and the Church both praising God. There are commentators who have created difficulties here by finding inconsistency. In verse 8, the praise of the living creatures is unceasing by day and night; in this passage, the picture is of separate bursts of praise at each of which the elders fall down and worship. But surely to say that there is an inconsistency is unimaginative criticism; we do not look for a strict logic in the poetry of adoration.

John uses a picture which the ancient world would know well. The elders cast their crowns before the throne of God. In the ancient world, that was the sign of complete submission. When one king surrendered to another, he cast his crown at the victor's feet. Sometimes the Romans carried with them an image of their emperor; and, when they had reduced a monarch to submission, there was a ceremony in which the vanquished one had to cast his crown before the emperor's image. The picture looks on God as the conqueror of human souls and on the Church as the body of people who have surrendered to him. There can be no Christianity without submission.

The doxology of the elders praises God on two counts.

(1) He is Lord and God. Here is something which would be even more meaningful to John's readers than it is to us. The phrase for Lord and God is *kurios kai theos*; and that was the official title of Domitian, the Roman emperor. It was, indeed, because the Christians would not acknowledge that claim that they were persecuted and killed. Simply to call God *Lord and*

God was a triumphant confession of faith, an assertion that God holds first place in all the universe.

(2) God is Creator. It is through his will and purpose that all things existed even before creation and were in the end brought into actual being. Human beings have acquired many powers, but we do not possess the power to create. We can alter and rearrange; we can make things out of already existing materials; but only God can create something out of nothing. That great truth means that in a very real sense everything in the world belongs to God, and there is nothing that we can handle which God has not given to us.

THE ROLL IN THE HAND OF GOD

Revelation 5:1

> And in the right hand of him who was seated on the throne I saw a roll written on the front and on the back, and sealed with seven seals.

WE must try to visualize the picture which John is drawing. It is taken from the vision of Ezekiel: 'I looked, and a hand was stretched out to me, and a written scroll was in it. He spread it before me; it had writing on the front and on the back, and written on it were words of lamentation and mourning and woe' (Ezekiel 2:9–10).

We must note that it was a *roll* and not a *book* which was in the hand of God. In the ancient world, down to the second century AD, literary works were in the form of a roll, not a book. The roll was made of papyrus, manufactured in single sheets about ten inches by eight. The sheets were joined together horizontally when a great deal of writing had to be done. The writing was in narrow columns about three inches long, with margins of about two and a half inches at the top and at the bottom, and with about three-quarters of an inch between the columns. The roll usually had a wooden roller at each end. It was held in the left hand, unrolled with the right, and, as the reading went on, the part in the left hand was rolled up again. We may get some idea of the dimensions of a roll from the following statistics. The books of 2 and 3 John, Jude and Philemon would each occupy one sheet of papyrus; Romans would require a roll 11½ feet long; Mark, 19 feet; John, 23½ feet; Matthew, 30 feet; Luke and Acts, 32 feet. Revelation itself would occupy a roll 15 feet long. It was such a roll that was in the hand of God. Two things are said about it.

(1) It was written *on the front and on the back*. Papyrus was a substance made from the pith of a bulrush which grew in the delta of the Nile. The bulrush was about fifteen feet high, with six feet of it below the water; and it was as thick as someone's wrist. The pith was extracted and cut into thin strips with a very sharp knife. A row of strips was laid vertically; on the top of them another row of strips was laid horizontally; the whole was then moistened with Nile water and glue and pressed together. The resulting substance was beaten with a mallet and then smoothed with pumice stone; and a substance emerged which was not unlike brown paper.

From this description, it will be seen that on one side the grain of the papyrus would run horizontally; that side was known as the *recto*; and on that side the writing was done, as it was easier to write where the lines of the writing ran with the lines of the fibres. The side on which the fibres ran vertically was called the *verso* and was not so commonly used for writing.

But papyrus was an expensive substance. So, if it was necessary to write a great deal, both the front and the back were written on. A sheet written on the back, the *verso*, was called an *opisthograph*, that is, a sheet written behind. The

Roman lawyer and satirist Juvenal talks of a young tragedian walking about with the papyrus manuscript of a tragedy on Orestes written on both sides; it was a lengthy production! The roll in God's hand was written on both sides; there was so much on it that both *recto* and *verso* were taken up with the writing.

(2) It was *sealed with seven seals*. That may indicate either of two things.

(a) When a roll was finished, it was fastened with threads which were then sealed at the knots. The one ordinary document sealed with seven seals was a will. Under Roman law, the seven witnesses to a will sealed it with their seals, and it could only be opened when all seven, or their legal representatives, were present. The roll may be what we might describe as God's will, his final settlement of the affairs of the universe.

(b) It is more likely that the seven seals stand simply for profound secrecy. The contents of the roll are so secret that it is sealed with seven seals. The tomb of Jesus was sealed to keep it safe (Matthew 27:66); the apocryphal Gospel of Peter says that it was sealed with seven seals. It was sealed in that way to make quite certain that no unauthorized person could possibly open it.

GOD'S BOOK OF DESTINY

Revelation 5:2–4

> And I saw a strong angel proclaiming in a great voice: 'Who is good enough to open the roll, and to loosen its seals?' And there was no one in heaven, or on earth, or under the earth, who was able to open the roll or to look at it; and I was weeping sorely because there was no

one who was found to be good enough to open the roll
or to see it.

As John looked at God with the roll in his hand, a challenge
came from a strong angel. A strong angel appears again in
10:1 and 18:21. In this case, the angel had to be strong so that
the challenge of his voice might reach throughout the universe.
His summons was that anyone worthy of the task should come
forward and open the book.

There is no doubt that the book is the record of what is
to happen in the last times. That there was such a book is a
common belief in Jewish thought. It is common in the Book
of Enoch. Uriel the archangel says to Enoch in the heavenly
places: 'O Enoch, observe the writing of the heavenly tablets,
and read what is written thereon, and mark every individual
fact.' Enoch goes on: 'And I observed everything on the
heavenly tablets, and read everything which was written
thereon, and understood everything, and read the book of
all the deeds of men and of all the children of flesh that
will be upon the earth to the remotest generations' (1 Enoch
81:1–2). In the same book, Enoch has a vision of the Head of
Days on the throne of his glory, 'and the books of the living
were opened before him' (1 Enoch 47:3). Enoch declares that
he knows the mystery of the holy ones, because 'the Lord
showed me and informed me, and I have read in the heavenly
tablets' (1 Enoch 106:19). On these tablets, he saw the history
of the generations still to come (1 Enoch 107:1). The idea is
that God has a book in which the history of time to come is
already written.

When we are seeking to interpret this idea, we should
always remember that it is vision and poetry. It would be
a great mistake to take it too literally. It does not mean that
everything has been settled long ago and that we are in the

grip of an inescapable fate. What it does mean is that God has a plan for the universe and that in the end the purpose of God will be worked out. As A. C. Ainger's hymn has it:

> God is working his purpose out, as year succeeds to year,
> God is working his purpose out, and the time is drawing near;
> Nearer and nearer draws the time, the time that shall surely be,
> When the earth shall be filled with the glory of God, as the waters cover the sea.

In response to the challenge of the angel, no one came forward; no one was good enough to open the roll. And, at this point in his vision, John begins to weep bitterly. There were two reasons for his tears.

(1) In 4:1, the voice had made the promise to him: 'I will show you what must take place after this.' It now looked as if the promise had been frustrated.

(2) There is a deeper reason for his sorrow. It seemed to him that there was no one in the whole universe to whom God could reveal his mysteries. Here, indeed, was a terrible situation. Many years before, Amos had said: 'Surely the Lord God does nothing, without revealing his secret to his servants the prophets' (Amos 3:7). But here was a world so far from God that no one was able to receive his message.

For John, that problem was to be solved triumphantly in the emergence of the Lamb. But behind this problem lies a great and a challenging truth. God cannot deliver a message to men and women unless they are able to receive it. This is the very essence of the problem of communication. It is the problem for teachers; they cannot teach truth which their students are unable to receive. It is the problem for preachers; they cannot deliver a message to a congregation totally incapable of comprehending it. It is the eternal problem of love; love cannot tell its truths or give its gifts to those incapable of hearing and receiving. The need of the world is for men and women who are sensitive to God. He has a message for the world in every generation; but that message cannot be delivered until people are found who are capable of receiving it. And, day by day, we either make ourselves receptive to the message of God or fail to hear it.

THE LION OF JUDAH AND THE ROOT OF DAVID

Revelation 5:5

> And one of the elders said to me: 'Stop weeping. Behold the Lion of the tribe of Judah, the Root of David, has won such a victory that he is able to open the book and its seven seals.'

WE are now approaching one of the most dramatic moments in Revelation – the emergence of the Lamb in the centre of the scene. Certain things lead up to it.

John has been weeping because there is no one to whom God may reveal his secrets. One of the elders, acting as the messenger of Christ, comes to him, saying: 'Do not weep.' These words were more than once on the lips of Jesus in the days of his earthly life. That is what he said to the widow of Nain when she was mourning her dead son (Luke 7:13), and to Jairus and his family when they were lamenting for their little girl (Luke 8:52). The comforting voice of Christ is still speaking in the heavenly places.

H. B. Swete makes an interesting comment on this passage. John was weeping, and yet his tears were unnecessary. Human grief often springs from insufficient knowledge. If we had patience to wait and trust, we would see that God has his own solutions for the situations which bring us tears.

The elder tells John that Jesus Christ has won such a victory that he is able to open the book and to loosen the seals. That means three things. It means that, because of his victory over death and all the powers of evil and because of his complete obedience to God, he is able to *know* God's secrets; he is able to *reveal* God's secrets; and it is his privilege and duty to *control* the things which shall be. Because of what Jesus did, he is the Lord of truth and of history. He is called by two great titles.

(1) He is the *Lion of Judah*. This title goes back to Jacob's final blessing of his sons before his death. In that blessing, he calls Judah 'a lion's whelp' (Genesis 49:9). If Judah himself is a lion's whelp, it is fitting to call the greatest member of the tribe of Judah *the Lion of Judah*. In the books written between the Testaments, this became a messianic title. One such book, 2 Esdras, speaks of the figure of a lion and says: 'This is the anointed one, that is, the Messiah' (2 Esdras [4 Ezra] 12:32). The lion's strength and its undoubted place as king of beasts make him a fitting emblem of the all-powerful Messiah whom the Jews awaited.

(2) He is the *Root of David*. This title goes back to Isaiah's prophecy that there will come forth a shoot from the stump of Jesse and a root of Jesse who shall be a signal to the people (Isaiah 11:1, 11:10). Jesse was the father of David, and this means that Jesus Christ was the Son of David, the promised Messiah.

So, here we have two great titles which are particularly Jewish. They have their origin in the pictures of the coming Messiah; and they lay it down that Jesus Christ triumphantly performed the work of the Messiah and is, therefore, able to know and to reveal the secrets of God, and to preside over the working out of his purposes in the events of history.

THE LAMB

Revelation 5:6

> And I saw a Lamb standing in the midst of the throne
> and of the four living creatures, and in the midst of the
> elders. It still bore the marks of having been slain. It had
> seven horns and seven eyes, which are the seven Spirits
> of God despatched to all the earth.

HERE is the supreme moment of this vision – the emergence
of the Lamb in the scene of heaven. It is possible to think of
this scene in two ways. Either we may think of the four living
creatures forming a circle around the throne and the twenty-
four elders forming a wider circle with a larger circumference,
with the Lamb standing between the inner circle of the four
living creatures and the outer circle of the twenty-four elders;
or, much more likely, the Lamb is the centre of the whole
scene.

The Lamb is one of the great characteristic ideas of
Revelation in which Jesus Christ is so named no fewer than
twenty-nine times. The word that John uses for *Lamb* is not
used of Jesus Christ anywhere else in the New Testament. John
the Baptist pointed to Jesus as the Lamb of God who takes
away the sin of the world (John 1:29, 1:36). Peter speaks of
the precious blood of Christ, as of a lamb without blemish
and without spot (1 Peter 1:19). In Isaiah 53:7, in the chapter
so dear to Jesus and to the early Church, we read of the lamb
brought to the slaughter. But, in all these cases, the word is
amnos, whereas the word that Revelation uses is *arnion*. This
is the word that Jeremiah uses, when he says: 'I was like a
gentle *lamb* led to the slaughter' (Jeremiah 11:19). By using
arnion and using it so often, John wants us to see that this is
a new idea which he is introducing.

(1) The Lamb still bears the marks of having been slain. There we have the picture of the sacrifice of Christ, still visible in the heavenly places. Even in the heavenly places, Jesus Christ is the one who loved us and gave himself for us.

(2) There is another side to this. This same Lamb, with the marks of sacrifice still on it, is the Lamb with the seven horns and the seven eyes.

(a) The seven horns stand for omnipotence, the possession of infinite power. In the Old Testament, the horn stands for two things.

First, it stands for sheer *power*. In the blessing of Moses, the horns of Joseph are like the horns of a wild ox, and with them he will drive the people to the ends of the earth (Deuteronomy 33:17). Zedekiah, the prophet, made iron horns as a sign of promised triumph over the Syrians (1 Kings 22:11). The wicked are warned: 'Do not lift up your horn' (Psalm 75:4). Zechariah sees the vision of the four horns which stand for the nations who have scattered Israel (Zechariah 1:18).

Second, it stands for *honour*. It is the confidence of the psalmist that in the favour of God our horn shall be exalted (Psalm 89:17). The horn of the good shall be exalted with honour (Psalm 112:9). God exalts the horn of his people (Psalm 148:14).

We must add still another strand to this picture. In the time between the Testaments, the great heroes of Israel were the Maccabees; they were the great warriors who were the liberators of the nations; and they are represented as horned lambs (1 Enoch 90:9).

Here is the great paradox: the Lamb bears the sacrificial wounds upon it; but at the same time it is clothed with the very might of God, which can now shatter its enemies. The Lamb has *seven* horns; the number *seven* stands for perfection; no one can withstand the power of the Lamb, which is perfect.

(b) The Lamb has seven eyes, and the eyes are the Spirits which are despatched into all the earth. The picture comes from Zechariah. There, the prophet sees the seven lamps which are 'the eyes of the Lord, which range through the whole earth' (Zechariah 4:10). It is an eerie picture; but quite clearly it stands for the omniscience of God, his infinite knowledge. In an almost crude way, it says that there is no place on earth which is not under the eye of God.

Here is a tremendous picture of Christ. He is the fulfilment of all the hopes and dreams of Israel, for he is the Lion of Judah and the Root of David. He is the one whose sacrifice was for the benefit of all people, and who still bears the marks of it in the heavenly places. But the tragedy has turned to triumph and the shame to glory; and he is the one whose all-conquering might no one can withstand and whose all-seeing eye no one can escape.

Few passages of Scripture show at one and the same time what Swete called 'the majesty and the meekness' of Jesus Christ and in the one picture combine the humiliation of his death and the glory of his risen life.

MUSIC IN HEAVEN

Revelation 5:7-14

> And the Lamb came and received the roll from the right hand of him who was seated on the throne. When it had received the roll, the four living creatures fell before the Lamb and so did the twenty-four elders, each of whom had a harp and golden bowls laden with incenses, which are the prayers of God's dedicated people. And they sang a new song and this is what they sang:
>
> Worthy are you to receive the roll and to open its seals, because you were slain, and so at the price of

your lifeblood you bought for God those of every tribe and tongue and people and race, and made them a kingdom of priests to our God, and they will reign upon the earth.

And I saw, and I heard the voice of many angels, who were in a circle round the throne, and the living creatures, and the elders; and their number was ten thousands of ten thousands and thousands of thousands; and they were singing with a great voice:

The Lamb which has been slain is worthy to receive the power and the riches and the wisdom and the strength and the honour and the glory and the blessing.

And I heard every created creature which was in the heaven, and upon the earth, and beneath the earth, and on the sea, and all things in them saying:

Blessing and honour. and glory and dominion for-ever and ever to him who sits upon the throne and to the Lamb.

And the four living creatures said: Amen; and the elders fell down and worshipped.

IT is necessary to look at this passage as a whole before we begin to deal with it in detail. R. H. Charles quotes the English poet Christina Rossetti on it: 'Heaven is revealed to earth as the homeland of music.' Here is the greatest chorus of praise the universe can ever hear. It comes in three waves. First, there is the praise of the four living creatures and of the twenty-four elders. Here, we see all nature and all the Church combining to praise the Lamb. Second, there is the praise of the great numbers of angels. Here is the picture of all the inhabitants of heaven lifting up their voices in praise. Third, John sees every creature, in every part of the universe, to its deepest depth and its furthest corner, singing in praise.

Here is the truth that heaven and earth and all that is within them are designed for the praise of Jesus Christ; and it is our privilege to lend our voices and our lives to this vast chorus of praise, for that chorus is inevitably incomplete as long as there is one voice missing from it.

THE PRAYERS OF THE SAINTS

Revelation 5:8

THE first section in the chorus of praise is the song of the four living creatures and the twenty-four elders; and, as we have seen, they represent all that is in nature and in the universal Church.

The picture of the elders is interesting. They have harps. The harp, or lyre, was the traditional instrument to which the Psalms were sung. 'Praise the Lord with the lyre; make melody to him with the harp,' says the psalmist (Psalm 33:2). 'Sing praises to the Lord with the lyre; with the lyre and the sound of melody' (Psalm 98:5). 'Sing to the Lord with thanksgiving; make melody to our God on the lyre' (Psalm 147:7). The harp, or lyre, stands for the music of praise as the Jews knew it.

The elders also have golden bowls full of incense; and the incense is the prayers of God's dedicated people. The likening of prayers to incense also comes from the Psalms. 'Let my prayer be counted as incense before you, and the lifting up of my hands as an evening sacrifice' (Psalm 141:2). But the significant thing is the idea of intermediaries in prayer. In later Jewish literature, this idea of heavenly intermediaries bringing the prayers of the faithful to God is very common. In the Testament of Dan (6:2), we read: 'Draw near to God and to the angel that intercedes for you, for he is a mediator between God and men.' In this literature, we find many such angels.

Chief of them all is Michael, the archangel, 'the merciful and long-suffering' (1 Enoch 40:9). He is said to come down daily to the fifth heaven to receive people's prayers and to bring them to God (3 Baruch 11). It is Gabriel who tells Enoch: 'I swear unto you that in heaven the angels remember you for good before the glory of the Great One' (1 Enoch 104:1). Sometimes it is the guardian angels who bring the prayers of men and women to God; and it is said that at certain times each day the doors are open so that the prayers may be received (Apocalypse of Paul 7:10). Sometimes all the angels, or, as Enoch calls them, the Watchers, are engaged in this task. It is to 'the Holy Ones of Heaven' that human souls complain with their cry for justice (1 Enoch 9:3). It is the duty of the Watchers of heaven to intercede for men and women (1 Enoch 15:2). As we have seen, the angels remember them for good (1 Enoch 104:1). Sometimes, it would seem, the blessed dead share in this task. The angels and the holy ones in their resting places make intercession (1 Enoch 39:5). There are certain things to be said about this belief in heavenly intermediaries.

(1) From one point of view, it is an uplifting thought. We are, so to speak, not left to pray alone. No prayer can be altogether heavy-footed and leaden-winged which has all the inhabitants of heaven behind it to help it rise to God.

(2) From another point of view, it is quite unnecessary. Before us is set an open door which no one can ever shut; no one's prayers need any assistance, for God's ear is open to catch the faintest whisper of appeal.

(3) The whole idea of intermediaries arises from a line of thought which we have met before. As the centuries went on, the Jews became increasingly impressed with the transcendence of God, his difference from human beings. They began to believe that there could never be any direct contact

between God and humanity and that there must be angelic intermediaries to bridge the gulf. That is exactly the feeling that Jesus Christ came to take away; he came to tell us that God 'is closer to us than breathing, nearer than hands or feet' and to be the living way by which for everyone, however humble, the door to God is open.

THE NEW SONG

Revelation 5:9

THE song that the four living creatures and the elders sang was a *new song*. The phrase *a new song* is very common in the Psalms; and there it is always a song for the new mercies of God. 'Sing to him a new song,' says the psalmist (Psalm 33:3). God took the psalmist out of the fearful pit and from the miry clay and set his foot on a rock and put a new song in his mouth to praise God (Psalm 40:3). 'O sing to the Lord a new song, for he has done marvellous things' (Psalm 98:1; cf. 96:1). 'I will sing a new song to you, O God' (Psalm 144:9). 'Praise the Lord! Sing to the Lord a new song, his praise in the assembly of the faithful' (Psalm 149:1). But the nearest parallel in the Old Testament comes from Isaiah. There, God declares new things, and the prophet calls upon people to sing to the Lord a new song (Isaiah 42:9–10).

The new song is always a song for new mercies of God; and it will be noblest of all when it is a song for the mercies of God in Jesus Christ.

One of the characteristics of Revelation is that it is the book of new things. There is the new name (2:17, 3:12), the new Jerusalem (3:12, 21:2), the new song (5:9, 14:3), the new heavens and the new earth (21:1); and there is the great promise that God makes all things new (21:5).

One most significant thing is to be noted. Greek has two words for *new*: *neos*, which means *new in point of time* but not necessarily in point of quality, and *kainos*, which means *new in point of quality*. *Kainos* describes a thing which has not only been recently produced but whose like has never existed before.

The significance of this is that Jesus Christ brings into life a quality which has never existed before – new joy, new thrill, new strength, new peace. That is why the supreme quality of the Christian life is a kind of brightness. It has been said that 'the opposite of a Christian world is a world grown old and sad'.

THE SONG OF THE LIVING CREATURES AND OF THE ELDERS

Revelation 5:9–10

> And they sang a new song and this is what they sang:
> Worthy are you to receive the roll and to open its seals, because you were slain, and so at the price of your lifeblood you bought for God those of every tribe and tongue and people and race, and made them a kingdom of priests to our God, and they will reign upon the earth.

THE praise offered to the Lamb by the four living creatures and the elders is given because he died. In this song, the results of the death of Jesus Christ are summed up.

(1) It was a *sacrificial* death. That is to say, it was a death with purpose in it. It was not an accident of history; it was not even the tragic death of a good and heroic man in the cause of righteousness and of God; it was a sacrificial death. The object of sacrifice is to restore the lost relationship between God and humanity; and it was for that purpose, *and with that result*, that Jesus Christ died.

(2) The death of Jesus Christ was a death which brought freedom. From beginning to end, the New Testament is full of the idea of the liberation achieved by him for all people. He gave his life as a ransom (*lutron*) for many (Mark 10:45). He gave himself as a ransom (*antilutron*) for all (1 Timothy 2:6). He redeemed us from – literally *bought us out from* (*exagorazein*) – the curse of the law (Galatians 3:13). We are redeemed (*lutrousthai*) not by any human wealth but by the precious blood of Jesus Christ (1 Peter 1:19). Jesus Christ is the Lord that bought us (*agorazein*) (2 Peter 2:1). We are bought with a price (*agorazein*) (1 Corinthians 6:20, 7:23). The New Testament consistently declares that it cost the death of Jesus Christ to rescue us from the dilemma and the slavery into which sin had brought us. The New Testament has no 'official' theory of how that effect was achieved; but of the effect itself it is in no doubt whatever.

(3) The death of Jesus Christ was *universal* in its benefits. It was for men and women of every race. There was a time when the Jews could hold that God cared only for them and wished for nothing but the destruction of other peoples. But in Jesus Christ we meet a God who loves *the world*. The death of Christ was for all people, and therefore it is the task of the Church to tell everyone about it.

(4) The death of Jesus Christ was a death which was of *benefit*. He did not die for nothing. In this song, three aspects of the work of Christ are singled out.

(a) He made us *royal*. He opened to men and women the royalty of the children of God. Human beings have always been God's children by creation; but now there is a new relationship of grace open to all.

(b) He made us *priests*. In the ancient world, only the priest had the right of approach to God. When ordinary Jews entered the Temple, they could make their way through the Court of the Gentiles, through the Court of the Women, into the Court of the Israelites; but into the Court of the Priests they could not go. It was a case of so far and no further. But Jesus Christ opened the way to God for all people. We all become priests in the sense that we have the right of access to God.

(c) He gave us *triumph*. His people shall reign upon the earth. This is not political triumph or material lordship. It is the secret of victorious living under any circumstances. 'In the world you face persecution. But take courage; I have conquered the world!' (John 16:33). In Christ, there is victory over self, victory over circumstance and victory over sin.

When we think of what the death and life of Jesus Christ have done for us, it is no wonder that the living creatures and the elders burst into praise of him.

THE SONG OF THE ANGELS

Revelation 5:11–12

> And I saw, and I heard the voice of many angels, who were in a circle round the throne, and the living creatures, and the elders; and their number was ten thousands of ten thousands and thousands of thousands; and they were singing with a great voice:
>
> The Lamb which has been slain is worthy to receive the power and the riches and the wisdom and the strength and the honour and the glory and the blessing.

THE chorus of praise is taken up by the countless hosts of the angels of heaven. They stand in a great outer circle round the throne and the living creatures and the elders, and they begin their song. We have repeatedly seen how John takes his language from the Old Testament; and here there is in his memory David's great thanksgiving to God:

Blessed are you, O Lord, the God of our ancestor Israel,
forever and ever. Yours, O Lord, are the greatness, the
power, the glory, the victory, and the majesty; for all
that is in the heavens and on the earth is yours; yours
is the kingdom, O Lord, and you are exalted as head
above all. Riches and honour come from you, and you
rule over all. In your hand are power and might; and it
is in your hand to make great, and to give strength to all.
(1 Chronicles 29:10–12)

The song of the living creatures and of the elders told of
the work of Christ in his death; now the angels sing of the
possessions of Christ in his glory. Seven great possessions
belong to the risen Lord.

(1) To him belongs the *power*. Paul called Jesus 'Christ the
power of God' (1 Corinthians 1:24). He is not one who can
plan but never achieve; to him belongs the power. We can say
triumphantly of him: 'He is able.'

(2) To him belong the *riches*. 'Though he was rich, yet for
your sakes he became poor' (2 Corinthians 8:9). Paul speaks
of 'the boundless riches of Christ' (Ephesians 3:8). There is
no promise that Jesus Christ has made that he does not possess
the resources to carry out. There is no claim on him which he
cannot satisfy.

(3) To him belongs the *wisdom*. Paul calls Jesus Christ 'the
wisdom of God' (1 Corinthians 1:24). He has the wisdom to
know the secrets of God and the solution of the problems of
life.

(4) To him belongs the *strength*. Christ is the strong one
who can disarm the powers of evil and overthrow Satan (Luke
11:22). There is no situation with which he cannot cope.

(5) To him belongs the *honour*. The day comes when to him
every knee shall bow and every tongue shall confess that he is
Lord (Philippians 2:11). A strange thing is that even those who

are not Christian often honour Christ by admitting that in his teaching alone lies the hope of this troubled world.

(6) To him belongs the *glory*. As John has it: 'We have seen his glory, the glory as of a father's only son, full of grace and truth' (John 1:14). Glory is that which by right belongs to God alone. To say that Jesus Christ possesses the glory is to say that he is divine.

(7) To him belongs the *blessing*. Here is the inevitable climax of it all. All these things Jesus Christ possesses, and every one of them he uses in the service of the men and women for whom he lived and died; he does not hold on to them for himself.

Therefore, thanksgiving for all that he has done rises to him from all the redeemed. And that thanksgiving is the one gift that we who have nothing can give to the one who possesses everything.

THE SONG OF ALL CREATION

Revelation 5:13-14

> And I heard every created creature which was in the heaven, and upon the earth, and beneath the earth, and on the sea, and all things in them, saying:
>
> Blessing and honour and glory and dominion forever and ever to him who sits upon the throne and to the Lamb.
>
> And the four living creatures said: Amen; and the elders fell down and worshipped.

Now the chorus of praise goes so far that it cannot go further, for it reaches throughout the whole of the universe and the whole of creation. There is one vast song of praise to the

Lamb. We may note one very significant thing. In this chorus of praise, God and the Lamb are joined together. Nothing could show the height of John's conception of Jesus Christ better than this. In the praise of creation, he sets him by the side of God.

In the song itself, there are two things to note.

The creatures which are in the heaven add their praise. Who are they? More than one answer has been given, and each is lovely in its own way. It has been suggested that the reference is to the birds of the air; the very singing of the birds is a song of praise. It has been suggested that the reference is to the sun, the moon and the stars; in their shining, the heavenly bodies are praising God. It has been suggested that the phrase gathers up every possible being in heaven – the living creatures, the elders, the great numbers of angels and every other heavenly being.

The creatures which are beneath the earth add their praise. That can only mean the dead who are in Hades – and here is something totally new. In the Old Testament, the idea is that the dead are separated altogether from God and from human beings and live a shadowy existence. 'For in death there is no remembrance of you; in Sheol who can give you praise?' (Psalm 6:5). 'What profit is there in my death if I go down to the Pit? Will the dust praise you? Will it tell of your faithfulness?' (Psalm 30:9). 'Do you work wonders for the dead? Do the shades rise up to praise you? Is your steadfast love declared in the grave, or your faithfulness in Abaddon? Are your wonders known in the darkness, or your saving help in the land of forgetfulness?' (Psalm 88:10–12). 'For Sheol cannot thank you, death cannot praise you; those who go down to the Pit cannot hope for your faithfulness' (Isaiah 38:18).

Here is a vision which sweeps all this away. Not even the land of the dead is beyond the reign of the risen Christ. Even from beyond death, the chorus of praise rises to him.

The picture here is an all-inclusive one of all nature praising God. There are in Scripture many magnificent pictures of the praise of God by nature. In the Old Testament itself, there is Psalm 148. But the noblest song of praise comes from the Apocrypha. In the Septuagint, there is an addition to Daniel. It is called *The Song of the Three Children*, and it is sung by Ananias, Azarias and Misael, as Shadrach, Meshach and Abednego are there called, before they enter the fiery furnace. It is long, but it is one of the world's great poems, and we must quote in full, in traditional language, the part in which they call on nature to praise God.

> O ye sun and moon, bless ye the Lord:
> Praise and exalt him above all for ever.
> O ye stars of heaven, bless ye the Lord:
> Praise and exalt him above all for ever.
> O every shower and dew, bless ye the Lord:
> Praise and exalt him above all for ever.
> O all ye winds, bless ye the Lord:
> Praise and exalt him above all for ever.
> O ye fire and heat, bless ye the Lord:
> Praise and exalt him above all for ever.
> O ye winter and summer, bless ye the Lord:
> Praise and exalt him above all for ever.
> O ye dews and storms of snow, bless ye the Lord:
> Praise and exalt him above all for ever.
> O ye nights and days, bless ye the Lord:
> Praise and exalt him above all for ever.
> O ye light and darkness, bless ye the Lord:
> Praise and exalt him above all for ever,
> O ye cold and heat, bless ye the Lord:
> Praise and exalt him above all for ever.
> O ye ice and cold, bless ye the Lord:
> Praise and exalt him above all for ever.
> O ye frost and snow, bless ye the Lord:

Praise and exalt him above all for ever.
O ye lightnings and clouds, bless ye the Lord:
Praise and exalt him above all for ever.
O let the earth bless the Lord:
Praise and exalt him above all for ever.
O ye mountains and little hills, bless ye the Lord:
Praise and exalt him above all for ever.
O all ye herbs of the field, bless ye the Lord:
Praise and exalt him above all for ever.
O all things that grow on the earth, bless ye the Lord:
Praise and exalt him above all for ever.
O ye fountains, bless ye the Lord:
Praise and exalt him above all for ever.
O ye seas and rivers, bless ye the Lord:
Praise and exalt him above all for ever.
O ye whales and all that move in the waters, bless ye
    the Lord:
Praise and exalt him above all for ever.
O all ye fowls of the air, bless ye the Lord:
Praise and exalt him above all for ever.
O all ye beasts and cattle, bless ye the Lord:
Praise and exalt him above all for ever.
O all ye creeping things of the earth, bless ye the
    Lord:
Praise and exalt him above all for ever.
O ye children of men, bless ye the Lord:
Praise and exalt him above all for ever.